11/12

D0461492

WITHDRAWN

GOD
*L*OVES
BROKEN
PEOPLE

(AND THOSE WHO PRETEND THEY'RE NOT)

SHEILA WALSH

THOMAS NELSON
Since 1798

NASHVILLE   DALLAS   MEXICO CITY   RIO DE JANEIRO

In memory of Ruth Bell Graham
who taught me to look for the beauty
that God hides in brokenness

Published in Nashville, Tennessee, by Thomas Nelson. Thomas Nelson is a trademark of Thomas Nelson, Inc.

The author is represented by the literary agency of Alive Communications, Inc., 7680 Goddard Street, Suite 200, Colorado Springs, Colorado 80920, www.alivecommunications.com.

Thomas Nelson, Inc., titles may be purchased in bulk for educational, business, fund-raising, or sales promotional use. For information, please e-mail SpecialMarkets@ThomasNelson.com.

Unless otherwise noted, Scripture quotations are taken from the HOLY BIBLE: NEW INTERNATIONAL VERSION®. Copyright © 1973, 1978, 1984 by International Bible Society. Used by permission of Zondervan Publishing House. All rights reserved.

Scripture quotations marked ESV are from THE ENGLISH STANDARD VERSION. Copyright © 2001 by Crossway Bibles, a division of Good News Publishers.

Scripture quotations marked NLT are from the *Holy Bible*, New Living Translation, copyright © 1996, 2001. Used by permission of Tyndale House Publishers, Inc., Wheaton, Illinois 60189. All rights reserved.

Scripture quotations marked JERUSALEM BIBLE are from THE JERUSALEM BIBLE. Copyright © 1966 by Darton, Longman & Todd Ltd. and Doubleday & Company, Inc. Used by permission.

Scripture quotations marked HCSB are from *Holman Christian Standard Bible*. Copyright © 1999, 2000, 2002, 2003 by Holman Bible Publishers, Nashville, Tennessee. All rights reserved.

Scripture quotations marked KJV are from the King James Version.

Scripture quotations marked NCV are from the New Century Version®. Copyright © 2005 by Thomas Nelson, Inc. Used by permission. All rights reserved.

Scripture quotations marked RSV are from the REVISED STANDARD VERSION of the Bible. Copyright © 1946, 1952, 1971, 1973 by the Division of Christian Education of the National Council of the Churches of Christ in the U.S.A. Used by permission.

Scripture quotations marked NASB are from the NEW AMERICAN STANDARD BIBLE®, © Copyright The Lockman Foundation 1960, 1962, 1963, 1968, 1971, 1972, 1973, 1975, 1977. Used by permission.

Other Scripture quotations are from *The Message* by Eugene H. Peterson, Copyright © 1993, 1994, 1995, 1996, 2000. Used by permission of NavPress Publishing Group. All rights reserved; J. B. Phillips: THE NEW TESTAMENT IN MODERN ENGLISH, Revised Edition. Copyright © J. B. Phillips 1958, 1960, 1972. Used by permission of Macmillan Publishing Co., Inc.

ISBN: 978-1-4041-8354-4 (IE)

Library of Congress Control Number: 2011945661

ISBN: 978-1-4002-0245-4

Printed in the United States of America

12 13 14 15 16 QGF 8 7 6 5 4 3 2 1

CONTENTS

CONTENTS

INTRODUCTION

It's Okay Not to Be Okay

I f I could write only one book in my lifetime, I would ask God to make it this one, the very book you now hold in your hands.

The message of this book is my life's passion. I believe with everything in me that God loves broken people, and that when somewhere in the painful process of that breaking and bruising we find a way to welcome Him into the darkness, we come to know His love in a way we have never known before.

And that, my friend, is no small thing.

When the glass house I had lived in for so many years came crashing to the ground, I began a new life outside the safety of those walls. No, it didn't feel good. Not at all. At first, it didn't even feel safe. But it felt *true*. I saw myself as a broken lamb limping after the Shepherd, not knowing where He was going but knowing that wherever He went, I would go with Him. To this very hour, I remain utterly convinced of one unalterable thing: the Shepherd loves me. The words I sang as a child feel more real to me today than ever: *Jesus loves me, this I know.*

I have seen this same conviction in the lives of other broken men and women I have met through the years. While they never would have signed up for the breaking (who would?), they would change nothing now. They wouldn't exchange the deeper relationship they have found with God for *anything*. It's not that God loves the broken among us more than those who perceive themselves as whole; it's simply that we *know* we are loved. We dare to believe it. And we know there is no hope, no life, and no ultimate meaning apart from Him.

I gave my life to Christ at age eleven. I am now fifty-five, and after forty-four years on this journey, I have invested my most strongly held and deeply felt beliefs in these pages.

That's not to say you'll find everything buttoned-down and tidy.

I would *like* to tell you that while everything used to be bad, now it's all good, and that all the scattered pages of my life's story have been tucked away in their proper pigeonholes.

But I can't tell you that.

Not yet.

Maybe not on this side of heaven.

Yes, I have days when the path ahead looks clear and I feel overwhelmed by the love and mercy of God. But I also have dark days and darker nights. . . .

One recurring dream haunts me. While the circumstances and characters change, the message always remains the same: *You are alone! You have always been alone, and you always will be alone.*

Most mornings I wake from this nightmare, shake off the worst of it, pour myself a cup of hot coffee, and embrace the new day. But sometimes the dream leaves dark little fingerprints, smudges not so easily brushed away that seem to cling to me for hours.

The dream has hounded me since childhood. I see myself walking down a corridor to an execution chamber, about to be put to death for a crime I did not commit. Through the glass walls of the corridor I can see family and friends talking to each other, laughing and telling stories. I cry out to them for help . . . but somehow, no one can hear me.

I wake up in a cold sweat. My husband lies beside me, my son sleeps soundly upstairs, and my dogs, one at my head and one on my feet, rest undisturbed. I feel the welcome weight of Belle across my ankles, tangible proof that I am *not* alone.

So why does the dream still stalk me, even after all these years? Old wounds, unfortunately, carry profound memories. In the moments just after I awake, pausing as my heartbeat returns to normal, I thank God that although I am not "fixed," I am loved.

It really is okay not to be okay.

Do you dare to believe that? Would you dare to bring all the broken pieces of your life—with the remnants of old wounds and stubborn nightmares—to God and let Him do what only He can do?

Many of us would willingly take such a dare . . . if only we could believe we are truly loved. So that is my prayer for you as we begin this journey together. I pray that you would know—down to the marrow of your bones— that God loves you with a fierce and undying passion, that you are not alone, and that He has committed Himself with all His omnipotent power to getting you safely all the way home.

I'M NOT WAVING; I'M DROWNING

When Deep Water Meets Even Deeper Love

She had struggled from childhood with overpowering feelings of melancholy.

As an adult, it was no better.

British poet Stevie Smith traced much of her struggle to a difficult childhood and to the devastation that swept over her after her father abandoned the family. Her most famous poem lent its title to a collection she published in 1957. She called it simply "Not Waving but Drowning."

Her brief, twelve-line poem pictures a dying man thrashing about in the surf, gesturing wildly, yet unable to attract the help of people passing by on the shore. The passersby see him, but they suppose he's merely waving. And so they walk on, maybe even waving back . . . leaving him to drown. The poem ends with these desolate lines:

> *I was much too far out all my life*
> *And not waving but drowning.*

Have you ever felt anything like that?

I have. Sometimes I still do.

Despite the fierce love of Jesus and the measureless grace of God, sometimes I thrust my hands up in the air, my arms flailing wildly, and people nod and smile and return what they see as a wave.

But I'm not waving. I'm drowning. Even for those of us who have walked with Christ for years, wounds from the past can still rush in like an unexpected storm.

In just the past couple of weeks, for example, the waters started to rise as I returned from a weekend speaking engagement. As is my custom, I texted my husband, "Landed!" when the wheels of the plane touched down on the tarmac. I've come to expect his return message, "Yay!" This time he added that he was picking up our son from a sleepover at his best friend's house.

At a little after 10:00 p.m. I retrieved my bag and headed out to my car. We live about thirty minutes from the airport, so I felt sure Barry and Christian would beat me home. As I turned into our driveway, however, the house was dark.

What a desolate feeling, seeing a dark house where I expected welcome lights flooding from the windows!

Oh well, I told myself. *It's probably taking longer than expected to retrieve Christian's stuff from places only teenage boys would think to leave them.* I shrugged off the small wave of fear and busied myself with unpacking.

By 11:00 p.m., however, I still hadn't heard anything.

I called Barry's cell, but he didn't pick up.

I texted him: "Where are you guys?" Nothing. No reply.

When by almost midnight I still hadn't heard anything, I felt the water rising over my head and the suffocating fingers of panic close in around my throat.

It's an all-too-familiar emotion. It's the hated voice way down in the cellar of my soul, whispering, *They're gone! You've always known it would happen one day. You lose what you love, Sheila. Always have, always will.*

I felt myself going under for the third time when a few moments later I finally heard Barry's car pull into the garage. It could have been—should have been—a moment of warmth and joy, a happy and relieved family reunion complete with a group hug.

But it wasn't.

Paralyzed by fear, instead of reaching out to my husband, I turned away, hiding in my own private cell. Instead of receiving a warm greeting from a wife deeply grateful he'd arrived home safely, my husband bore the silence of questions I didn't know how to ask. When I did find a voice, I threw my questions randomly into the air, meaning them as flares—but they stung like arrows.

I have often found anger more comfortable than fear. Anger gives me the illusion of control, while fear leaves me naked and exposed.

When the waves finally subsided, I found myself in a puddle of shame. *Why did I react like that?*

Have I learned nothing over the years?
How could I lose my footing so quickly?

Barry had stayed with friends longer than expected to talk with them about a distressing storm of their own. He had also thought I might appreciate a little time to myself after a tiring weekend. Now, wasn't that ironic? I had just returned from telling ten thousand women that Christ offers peace in the fiercest storm—and now my own words battered me.

I'm not waving; I'm drowning.

Unlearning Old Lessons

Over the years I've learned that while Jesus' love remains constant, our *experience* of that love does not. That's a big problem for many of us because we grew up thinking that once we learned whatever lessons God wanted to teach us, we could sail through life triumphantly on a golden cloud, regardless of the serious challenges or difficulties that knocked on (or knocked down) our doors. Maybe you have pleaded with God, as I have, "Lord, I've learned this lesson. I really have! So can't we move on? *Please?*"

"Moving on," however, isn't always an option. Life is what it is, our challenges are what they are, and the big changes we long for so intently may take place *within* us, rather than *around* us in our circumstances. It's taken me a while to "get" that lesson.

Truth be told, I'm still learning.

On the other hand, please don't imagine that my life swings wildly from the highest of highs to the lowest of lows. Actually, some of the situations in which I find myself can even seem quite funny—at least, after a little time has passed.

A few years ago I received an invitation to take part in a crusade in London, England. Pastor Paul Yonggi Cho from Seoul, South Korea, would do the main speaking while I would do the singing. Since I love any opportunity to return to my homeland, I felt excited that the event would take place in the magnificent new twenty-thousand-seat O2 arena. I flew in the day before, and as we drove to the hotel, I asked the local event planner when I could do a sound check. He said he would take me over to the venue the following afternoon.

When the knock came at my door at 3:00 p.m., I quickly grabbed my things, ready to leave for the arena. But it wasn't the event planner at my door; it was a small greeting committee. They said they had just come from Dr. Cho's room and would like to come in and chat for a few moments. I invited them in, and after an awkward silence, one man cleared his throat and declared there had been a "slight change of plan."

In retrospect, it would have been like one of the sailors on Jonah's storm-tossed ship telling the prophet, "There is a little fish just over the side of the boat who would love to say hello."

They told me that rather than promote the event themselves, they had hoped *God* would do the promoting. But apparently He hadn't. The gentleman explained that because of the change in circumstances, there would be a change of venue. Instead of meeting at the O2 Arena, we would hold forth at Peckham High School. (That's like going from the Cowboys Stadium in Dallas, Texas, to your local 7-Eleven.)

"That's absolutely fine with me," I replied.

But I spoke too soon.

"Well," he continued, "we were hoping you wouldn't mind going over to the arena and standing outside with a sign saying the event's been moved— just in case anyone shows up. Just wave it as high as you can!"

Am I hearing this correctly?

I politely declined that opportunity and settled instead for singing through a bullhorn in the school gym!

Horrifying at the time, but quite funny today.

What's It Doing in God's Word?

Let's admit right now that a lively wave of the hand often doesn't mean "Hello!"

Sometimes it can mean "Help!"

I think this is especially true when life fails to turn out like we thought it would. Perhaps we began our Christian lives with great dreams, soaring hopes, and fervent anticipation. But somewhere down the line, our dreams decayed, our hopes got hammered, and our anticipation all but vanished into the abyss. Crushed expectations can leave us feeling desperate, despairing, and desolate.

Have you ever read Psalm 88?

It isn't likely you will see the words of this psalm on a wall plaque or in a framed cross-stitch in the family room. This "psalm of lament" could give even psalms of lament a bad name. While most such songs start out with some kind of desperate plea—"How long, O LORD? Will you forget me forever?"—they normally end in praise or at least with a little hope: "I will sing to the LORD, for he has been good to me" (Psalm 13:1, 6).

Not so in Psalm 88.

Yes, it definitely opens with a plea for help—"Day and night I cry out before you. May my prayer come before you; turn your ear to my cry." But you will look in vain at the end of the song for praise, for hope, or even for a *teensy* bit of light. The writer describes God's "wrath" sweeping over him and the Lord's "terrors" destroying him, surrounding him, completely engulfing him. And then comes verse 18:

> You have taken my companions and loved ones from me;
> the darkness is my closest friend.

And that's it. End of psalm. Period.

When was the last time you saw anyone use *that* verse to conclude a worship service? I never have, and I'm pretty sure you haven't either.

So why did God include Psalm 88 in His Word? Why is it even *there*? Do we have so little hardship and pain in this life that we have to read about it in the Scriptures?

I told you in this book's introduction that I wouldn't offer you a nice, tidy system of belief that heals all wounds, brings out the sunshine, or inspires the angels to thunder the Hallelujah Chorus. The truth is, I think Psalm 88 has a place in our Bibles because it's *true*. It reflects how we feel sometimes—yes, even those who have a passionate love for Christ.

Do you *feel* as though God's wrath has withered you, whether for some good reason or for no reason at all? So did the psalmist.

Do you *feel* as though His terrors are destroying you, surrounding you, completely engulfing you? So did the psalmist.

Do you *feel* as though all your loved ones and companions have been snatched from you? So did the psalmist.

Does the darkness *feel* like your closest friend? It certainly did for the psalmist.

In chapter 6, we'll discuss some ways to deal with dark feelings such as this, but for now I just want you to recognize that God knows such feelings exist, *and He chose to honor them by including a record of them in His Holy Word*.

Why? Because those are words that may come from our own hearts someday, if they haven't already. What's more, "He knows our frame; he remembers that we are dust" (Psalm 103:14 ESV). Don't make the common mistake of trying to deny your feelings or pretending they don't matter or feeling guilty and condemned because you have them. While I don't counsel you to wallow in them, neither do I suggest that you hide from them or run away from them.

Listen to one of my favorite quotes from Shakespeare's profoundly tragic tale *King Lear*:

> *The weight of this sad time we must obey;*
> *Speak what we feel, not what we ought to say.*

Remember this: God sees your arms flailing, and He knows very well that you're not waving; you are going under for the third time. As the ultimate Lifeguard, He's seen a lot of thrashing arms in the wild surf of life:

- MOSES—"If this is how you are going to treat me, put me to death right now . . . and do not let me face my own ruin" (Numbers 11:15).
- JOB—"Why then did you bring me out of the womb? I wish I had died before any eye saw me" (Job 10:18).
- DAVID—"What gain is there in my destruction, in my going down into the pit?" (Psalm 30:9).
- JONAH—"Now, O LORD, take away my life, for it is better for me to die than to live" (Jonah 4:3).
- ELIJAH—"I have had enough, LORD. . . . Take my life; I am no better than my ancestors" (1 Kings 19:4).
- THE DISCIPLES—"Teacher, don't you care if we drown?" (Mark 4:38).
- PAUL—"We despaired even of life. Indeed, in our hearts we felt the sentence of death" (2 Corinthians 1:8–9).
- JESUS"—My God, my God, why have you forsaken me?" (Matthew 27:46).

Drowning, indeed.

Broken Pieces

Early in the morning I love to take a mug of good, strong coffee out onto the patio and watch the sun rise. Our home backs onto a lake, and the beautiful scenery changes with the seasons. For all the loveliness and color of that scene, however, my gaze always returns to a certain stone . . . a mosaic stone at the edge of our lawn. With its garishly bright colors and uneven shapes, you might think it looks a little out of place. But I consider it a priceless treasure.

I remember the morning that my son, Christian, then seven years old, gave the stone to me. I remember it well for two reasons. First, this beautiful homemade gift came from the heart of my little boy, and, second, he almost collapsed my lungs when he thrust it upon me!

As my birthday approached, Christian told his dad he wanted to make something special for me. After considering a number of ideas, they finally settled on a project Christian had seen advertised in a magazine—a mosaic stepping-stone kit. The magazine showed a picture of a beautiful finished piece, and I think Christian imagined that's what he was ordering. So when the kit arrived and he opened it up, he felt very disappointed.

"Look, Dad, it's just a box of broken things. I can't give *that* to Mom!"

Barry explained that Christian would use the pieces to create his own pattern to make a one-of-a-kind gift. Once he caught a glimpse of the plan, Christian *really* liked that idea. For the next few days, the boys banned me from the guest bedroom, where they'd spread out the materials over a large towel until they could complete the masterpiece. Barry told our young son that he should pick and choose which pieces to use, but Christian felt determined to work in every single piece from the box. His creation wound up in poured concrete, so the finished product weighed a ton.

On the morning of my birthday, Christian came staggering into our bedroom, carrying his gift in a box. He asked me to close my eyes and hold out my hands. I closed my eyes and prepared to hold out my hands, but when his gift got too heavy for him, he unloaded it onto my chest. It almost flattened me! We took the stone outside that very morning and placed it right at the edge of the lawn by the patio, and even today that's the first thing you see when you set foot outside.

I love that stepping-stone.

I love the way Christian arranged all the pieces, giving prominence to purple, my favorite color. What I love even more is that just before the concrete set, he wrote in it, "I love you, Mom" with his little finger.

One morning as I sat outside, gazing at the stone glimmering in the early light, Christian came out and joined me. Out of the blue, he asked a question:

"Mom, do you think someone broke the pieces on purpose, or do you think they just gathered up broken things and used them?"

I answered that I imagined they collected broken things, but his question stayed with me for a long time. In fact, I still ponder it.

I think about all the broken pieces of my life and in the lives of those I love, the men and women I've encountered in my ministry. And I've asked God, "Father, do You orchestrate the breaking of our lives, or just invite us to bring all the pieces to You?"

Thinking about my question has led to another: Does it matter? Would we relate to God any differently depending on His answer?

It's one thing to love God when we think of Him as the One who binds up our brokenness. But what if He is the One who allows, even participates, in the breaking?

Where Is God?

I sat outside again this morning, looking at my stepping-stone and praying for some of my friends who currently suffer heartache and pain and brokenness. Two of them are embroiled in a bitter divorce; one spouse wants it; the other doesn't. I see so much hurt and anger there. I care deeply for both of them, but I can do nothing to help. I listen and weep and pray, but I can't fix their problems. I can't restore their marriage, undo the wrong turns made along the way, or bring healing to their hearts.

Over the years I have talked to many with failing marriages. So often they ask me,

"Why won't God change my husband's heart?"

"If God hates divorce so much, why won't He help me rebuild our relationship?"

"I don't want my kids to be a statistic, coming from one more broken family. I feel so helpless!"

Hands up, Arms thrashing Not waving
Drowning.

Another dear friend struggles with brain cancer. He has an amazing family, each member rock-solid in the faith. But his three young boys wonder what on earth is going on and ask some very valid questions.

"Does God hear our prayers?"

"Why won't He heal my dad?"

"Is my dad going to die?"

Not waving. Drowning.

My friends who wrestle with infertility ask another set of questions. So do those who struggle with joblessness, financial ruin, or bankruptcy. Others, even in adulthood, continue to try to overcome the wounds of childhood abuse, neglect, or abandonment. Whatever the heartache, the questions ultimately sound the same:

"Where are You, God?" (or "Where *were* You?")

"Don't You see my pain?"

"You say You love me. Then how can You leave me like this? How can You turn away?"

"Why won't You do *something*????"

With raised and frightened voices we continue to ask the shrill question of the disciples, foundering on a waterlogged boat while their Messiah slumbered on: "Teacher, don't You care if we drown?"

Could you be asking that question right now?

Will He Pick Up the Phone?

Years ago a frantic man drove his sick wife hundreds of miles to visit *The 700 Club* (a daily religious program on the Christian Broadcasting Network), hoping that the prayers of televised saints would do more good for his sweetheart than had his own tearful petitions. He apparently believed, as many do, that the moderately famous have better connections to heaven than do the seemingly anonymous.

More than one woman has said to me something like, "Sheila, God is more likely to pick up the phone when you call than when I do." These women really believe, *God is connected to you, but not to me.*

One distraught woman bitterly roasted me for several minutes over my "perfect son" (her words). She let me know in no uncertain terms that she felt sick of me talking about his successes and was fed up with hearing about his marvelous spiritual growth. She despised these stories and hated every triumphant detail.

And then she broke down and wept. Her own son had died unexpectedly, and she just couldn't bear the thought that God might spare one mother's heart but shatter her own. Her bitter disappointment with God over the loss of her son just couldn't help spilling over into every other part of her life.

That was a broken woman, a woman for whom Christ died and whom God loved so much that He sent His own Son to Calvary that He might prepare the salve that heals broken hearts. It sounds good, doesn't it? It has the ring of truth. We like the idea of a Savior-made potion powerful enough to mend our shattered, broken hearts.

But we despise the brokenness itself.

Oh, we may mouth the well-known verses about "all have sinned" and "all we like sheep have gone astray" (KJV)—but generally we would rather not ponder, let alone deal with, the kind of desperate brokenness that our sin has bequeathed to us.

But what is the alternative? Bitterness, like the woman with the dead son? Guilt, like the man with the diseased wife? Deep self-doubt, like the women who believed they had malfunctioning telephone lines?

Or an agonized death grip on the promises of the Lord, like the crucified and broken Son of God?

You may know that when Jesus cried out on the cross, "My God, my God, why have you forsaken me?" His words echoed Psalm 22:1, a prophecy of David about the Lord's crucifixion, given more than a thousand years before Christ's death. While that's remarkable enough, keep in mind that Jesus didn't merely quote these words from the cross in order to fulfill prophecy. No! Those words were torn from the very core of His soul—tortured, sorrowful, troubled, tormented. The very skies turned black for the horror of what was happening.

We don't know exactly what mysterious divine transaction took place in those dark hours, nor will we likely ever know. Somehow, as Christ took on Himself all the sins of the world, the Father looked away—and so the blessed Savior screamed His wail of abandonment as He was plunged into darkness that we will never know.

But then the moment passed, as all moments do.

And with Roman spikes still piercing His hands and feet and with His flowing blood still staining the wood of the cross and the dust of the earth, the real agony—the spiritual and emotional agony—abated. In His last moments, Jesus forgave a thief and made arrangements for the care of His mother. He cried out, "It is finished!" He had drained every last drop from the cup of the wrath of God and now commended His spirit into the care of His heavenly Father.

What gave Him the strength to recover like that? While I can't prove it, I think He did more than quote the first line of Psalm 22 in His darkest hour (an hour far, *far* darker than the blackest night we have ever known or will ever know). I think He mentally worked His way through the whole psalm.

When we look at Psalm 22, many of us may focus on the startling prophecies that came so literally true at the crucifixion: Jesus' cry of desperation and abandonment (v. 1), the taunts and jeers of His cruel opponents (vv. 6–7), the description of what happens physically to a man crucified (vv. 14–15), the piercing of Christ's hands and feet (v. 16), the casting of lots for His clothing (v. 18). We breathe a sigh of astonishment, and then we turn the page.

But we turn too quickly.

I believe that as Jesus continued to hang on the cross, He worked His way through the rest of this psalm, whose verses imply His resurrection (v. 22), the birth of the worldwide church (v. 27), and His ultimate reign over all the earth (vv. 30–31). What kept our Lord going until the very end? How did He move from feelings of abandonment to utter confidence in the warm, welcoming, loving embrace of His Father?

As He did all of His life, Jesus laid hold of the promises and the truth of God's Word.

I want you to know that for the rest of this book, I'll be telling a lot of stories and incidents from my life and from the lives of others, all in the desire to show you—and God helping me, *convince* you—of the hope we have in Christ Jesus no matter how broken we are. But remember as you read that none of these stories can do for you what the Word of God can do. And that is why I intend to root everything I say in the Scriptures.

I love what author and pastor John Piper wrote at the beginning of

Desiring God. He said that if he could not show that his teaching came from the Bible, "I do not expect anyone to be interested, let alone persuaded." I *really* like that! And I also agree with his next statement: "There are a thousand man-made philosophies of life. If this is another, let it pass. There is only one rock: the Word of God."[1]

As we walk the rest of this journey together, I'd like you to train your eyes on two crucial things: one ancient, one new. The prophet Jeremiah gives us the ancient bit of this wonderful pair:

> This is what the LORD says:
> "Stand at the crossroads and look;
>   ask for the ancient paths,
> ask where the good way is, and walk in it,
>   and you will find rest for your souls."
>
> (JEREMIAH 6:16)

This "ancient path" and "good way" is nothing other than the Word of God, the Bible. Throughout this book you and I will return constantly to its wisdom and lean on its counsel, for if we want rest for our souls, that is the place to find it. (There is a companion Bible Study at the end of this book so that together we can dive deeper into the life-saving Word of God.)

Do you remember Stevie Smith, the poet who wrote "Not Waving but Drowning"? So far as we know, she never found the rest for her soul that she so desperately sought her whole life. She waved and she waved, and then she drowned. Clive James said of her, "Her poems, if they were pills to purge melancholy, did not work for her."[2] Words, no matter how potent, simply lack the spiritual muscle to give our souls rest.

For that, we need more than poetry or philosophy or human wisdom; we need the living, breathing Word of God.

Isaiah gives us the second hook on which to hang our hats. Not only do we rest on the solid rock of the Word of God, but we are called to open our eyes and see what God is doing in us and preparing for us right now! God speaks through the prophet to tell us,

> See, I am doing a new thing!
> Now it springs up; do you not perceive it?

I am making a way in the desert
and streams in the wasteland.

(ISAIAH 43:19)

Too often when we feel as though we're about to drown, we let our focus lock onto life's rearview mirror. We see so clearly our mistakes, our obvious wrong turns, our skewed perspective, and the unhappy turns of events that mark our personal history.

That's the way it looks . . . in the rearview mirror.

But who can drive anywhere looking in the rearview mirror? That mirror has been strategically placed over the windshield so our eyes can catch a quick glimpse of All Things Behind, before we return our gaze to All Things Ahead. We glance at the road behind, but we fix our eyes on the road before us.

Some of us allow our hurtful past to absorb us, consume us, and hold us back. Whether we run from our past or live in our past, it continues to control us.

But no one can drive that way . . . or live that way.

God says to you and me, "It's time for something new in your life. I open up new roads before you. I want to fill the desert of your soul with living water and satisfy your thirst with heaven's swift, cool brooks. Don't dwell on the past, and refuse to camp in the tragedies of your history or family background. Leave it all behind! And then come with Me, for I have something brand-new in mind for you."

So with one hand firmly gripping the Word of God, and the other hand reaching for the fresh future God is busily at work preparing for us, let us walk together on this journey into God's best. It may be hard, but it will be worth it.

Bummer Lambs and Black Sheep

A Shepherd Who Pursues Both Victims and Villians

From time to time I get asked to read other authors' manuscripts to see if I would consider writing an endorsement. I really enjoy the process when I know the author personally—it excites me to get a sneak peek at his or her latest project—and reading the book feels like listening to him or her over a cup of coffee. I can hear my friend's voice as I read.

But every so often I receive a manuscript from someone I've never met or even heard of. In those cases, if I get drawn in at all, it's because of the subject matter or possibly an intriguing title. That's what happened when my assistant handed me a copy of *Heaven Has Blue Carpet*.

I like that sort of title. You find yourself just naturally responding, "It does? Heaven has carpet? And the carpet's blue? Who knew?"

Actually, I couldn't imagine where the title came from, but felt pretty sure it wasn't from the book of Revelation. As I dived into Sharon Niedzinski's story, I found myself by turns laughing out loud and pausing to reflect on the deeper observations of this suburban housewife on her journey to become— of all things—a shepherd!

Sharon, her husband, and their six children left their predictable, comfortable lives, moved into a dilapidated old farmhouse, and began the process of learning to care for sheep. I loved reading about their adventures and gladly endorsed this well-written book. Sharon's take on the spiritual truths and life lessons we can learn from the lives of shepherds and their sheep intrigued me.

In her book, Sharon tells of a ewe that gave birth to triplets, but accepted only two of the lambs. When the third lamb tried to approach its mother for milk, she butted it out of the way. Sharon and her family did everything they could think of to get the ewe to accept the third lamb, but she refused, stamping her feet and kicking at the newborn. Nothing can change a stubborn ewe's mind!

At one point Sharon saw the little lamb with its head bowed over and thought it had injured its neck. But further investigation revealed no physical injuries. It was the lamb's spirit that had been broken.

Sharon soon discovered that what happened to this little lamb occurred fairly often. Sometimes a mother ewe dies, leaving the lamb an orphan; or a first-time mother becomes overwhelmed and chooses to ignore her baby rather than face the challenge of caring for it. Or as in the case of the ewe on Sharon's farm, a sheep that cannot produce enough milk for multiple offspring will choose to feed some and reject others. These abandoned, rejected lambs are called "bummer lambs."

All too often, these needy, vulnerable, precious lambs simply die. Their little spirits break, and they give up the will to live. The only ones who do survive—the ones who find the strength to overcome their mother's rejection—are the ones who get taken in and cared for by the shepherd.

Sharon and her family took "Joey," their rejected lamb, into their home. Joey, the bummer lamb, became Joey, a blessed lamb, as he was surrounded by people who nurtured him, fed him, watched over him, and protected him. He learned to walk on the blue carpet in the living room of Sharon's home—heaven to this little bummer lamb.

Later, when Joey grew strong enough to return to the grassy pasture, he struggled at first. What was this funny green stuff? It didn't feel right at all! Joey felt most at home on soft blue carpet.

From this unique experience, Sharon made a powerful observation: bummer lambs are in fact the most blessed of all the sheep in the pasture because they are the most personally and intimately cared for by the shepherd. They develop a kind of relationship with the shepherd that other sheep can't even dream of. They experience a love that far surpasses anything the pasture and sometimes-fickle ewe have to offer.

When the shepherd calls to the flock, guess who run to him first?

The bummer lambs!

Why? Because they know his voice best, and they have been held close to his heart. It's not that he loves them more; it's just that they've been broken enough to let that love in . . . down deep.

God's Bummer Lambs

In a spiritual sense, we're all "bummer lambs"—lost in sin, broken in spirit, wounded in heart and mind . . . and sometimes body. Many of us have felt like bummer lambs in our family of origin or even (sad to say) in the family of God. We know what it means to feel unwanted and unloved, pushed out of the way, abandoned, rejected, abused, or neglected.

Happily for us, Scripture often calls God a Shepherd, with us as His sheep. So the psalmist said, "He brought me out into a spacious place; he rescued me because he delighted in me" (Psalm 18:19).

The good news is that no matter what we've suffered in the past or no matter how dark the valley we find ourselves in today—whether our brokenness results from what others have done to us or what we have done to ourselves—we have a heavenly Shepherd who cares for us deeply and loves us fiercely. The prophet Isaiah tells us that God "tends his flock like a shepherd: He gathers the lambs in his arms and carries them close to his heart; he gently leads those that have young" (Isaiah 40:11).

If you feel like a bummer lamb, understand that when Isaiah says the Lord "gathers" you in His arms, he uses a Hebrew term that most often refers to assembling people into one place. It speaks of a sovereign, intentional act. He looked for *you*, and when He found you, He scooped you up into His arms and placed you safely and securely among His own flock. You weren't an afterthought. You weren't simply in the right place at the right time to catch His eye. No, in His love and in His majesty He searched for you, picked you out, picked you up, and held you firmly in His arms.

But He didn't stop there!

Note that Isaiah says He carries you "close to his heart." Edward Young, an Isaiah scholar, wrote about this verse,

> In verse 10 there had already been mention of His arm as ruling for Him. This *arm* is the symbol of His might and power and is sufficiently strong to gather up the sheep for protection and care. When they are in the Shepherd's arm, nothing can harm or come near to separate them from Him. Those whom He gathers are described as lambs, i.e. the young lambs recently born. They are the weakest members of the flock, which cannot possibly defend themselves against attack and which are in need of the Shepherd's

constant protection. By means of His arm He will gather them up, and in His bosom He will carry them so that they will recline in His arm against His bosom. Thus they will not have to walk themselves nor stumble nor go astray.[4]

This divine Shepherd searches the hills looking for us, day and night. He scoops us up and carries us in His arms until we grow strong enough to walk. He even adopts us into His family!

How tenderly He works.

How gently He deals with the bruised and broken.

Isaiah said of Him, "A bruised reed he will not break, and a smoldering wick he will not snuff out" (Isaiah 42:3).

Do you feel like a bruised reed—wounded, bent over, ready to snap in two at the slightest breeze? Your Shepherd sees your precarious condition, and He will never break you. He desires, rather, to bind up your wounds.

Maybe you feel more like a smoldering wick—spent, burned out, and little more than a wispy curl of sooty smoke? Your Shepherd promises that He will never snuff you out. His caring hands will gently attend to your injuries and keep your flame alive, weak as it may be.

Of course, that doesn't mean you'll walk through life pain-free. He *never* promised that! When the Lord told us that He sent Jesus "to bind up the brokenhearted" (Isaiah 61:1), He used the Hebrew word *chavash*, which means "to bind on, wrap around; bind up as a wound, bandage, cover, envelop, enclose." A broken heart bleeds, and the only way to stop the bleeding is to compress the wound. God applies pressure exactly at the injured spot—not to make it hurt, but to stop the flow of blood.

Beth Moore wrote, "What a wonderful picture of Christ! A crushing hurt comes, and the sympathizing, scarred hand of Christ presses the wound; and for just a moment, the pain seems to intensify . . . but finally the bleeding stops."[4]

Jesus clearly was thinking of passages like these from Isaiah, or others like Psalm 147:3—"He heals the brokenhearted and binds up their wounds"—when He revealed Himself as the Good Shepherd (John 10). And what does the Good Shepherd do? He calls to His sheep, by name, and they come to Him. He leads them out to find food and water. He goes ahead of them to scout out the territory, to make sure they will remain safe and well nurtured. He brings in all the sheep that belong to Him, from whatever fold. And He gives them all life, abundant life—in fact, He lays down His *own* life so that they might participate in the fullness of His life.

And for what sort of sheep does Jesus do all this? The prizewinners? The prime ewes and the proud rams? The sheep with the thickest wool, brightest eyes, and strongest limbs?

No, He does it for stumbling, wandering, weak sheep. He does it for bummer lambs, like you and me. And He has great things in store for His flock: "When the Chief Shepherd appears, you will receive the crown of glory that will never fade away" (1 Peter 5:4).

And even then, at the very end of time, this Good Shepherd, this Great Shepherd, this Chief Shepherd, will not cease to take tender and meticulous care of His bummer lambs. John tells us that many of His sheep will have to endure much in this life and on this fallen earth. But in the end . . .

> *They are before the throne of God*
> > *and serve him day and night in his temple;*
> > *and he who sits on the throne will spread his tent over them.*
> *Never again will they hunger;*
> > *never again will they thirst.*
> *The sun will not beat upon them,*
> > *nor any scorching heat.*
> *For the Lamb at the center of the throne will be their shepherd;*
> > *he will lead them to springs of living water.*
> *And God will wipe away every tear from their eyes.*

(REVELATION 7:15–17)

Black Sheep

You might say to me, "Sheila, that is so beautiful. And it's wonderful. But you just don't understand. I'm not a bummer lamb; if anything, I'm a black sheep. I have wandered away from the Good Shepherd more times than I can count. I have refused His arms and instead have run into the arms of those who only wanted to use and abuse me. I'm spent. I have nothing left. What you say sounds marvelous, but it just doesn't apply to me."

Forgive me, but I'm quite sure you're wrong.

You see, the Bible doesn't talk about "white sheep"—or "black sheep" either, for that matter. In fact, the only color it seems to assign to God's sheep is crimson—a deep, purplish-red. But don't take my word for it. Listen to God Himself:

> "Come now, let us reason together,"
> says the LORD.
> "Though your sins are like scarlet,
> they shall be as white as snow;
> though they are red as crimson,
> they shall be like wool."

(ISAIAH 1:18)

Just as all of us qualify in some ways as bummer lambs, so all of us qualify in all ways as what we call black sheep. But your sin—no matter how dark a stain you think it has left—can never keep you apart from God. Only your stubborn will can do that. He says to you, "Come." Yes, He says it to *you*, even you of the black wool. Even you of the wandering hooves. And when you come, He knows how to take any color of wool and turn it into clean, bright, white-as-snow wool.

Even yours.

As I write these words, a passionate confidence grows stronger and stronger within me. In many ways it's been my life message, but it burns in me now as never before.

Just as you are, right now, with all the choices you have made, both good and bad, on your best days and your worst, with all the deepest, darkest secrets of the heart you have ever confessed to our Father, as well as those you still try to hide—*you are loved by God with a fiery love that will never fail.*

Can you receive this truth, even if you feel like a black sheep? Can you receive it, even if you feel yourself to be a shame and a disgrace? Can you receive it, even if you have failed miserably and by your behavior disappointed everyone around you?

If you struggle to say yes, then let me remind you of a parable Jesus once told. He spoke of a man who owned a hundred sheep. When one of them wandered away, he left the ninety-nine on the hills to go out and search for one lost sheep—you know, the one who left all the "good" and "white" sheep to wander away. Do you recall what this man did when he found his lost sheep (whether it had black, white, or plaid wool, we're not told)? Jesus said that he rejoiced over it *more than over the ninety-nine who didn't wander away* (see Matthew 18:12–13).

If you study the Gospel accounts, you'll find this story in Luke as well, with one interesting difference. In Matthew's version, the missing sheep represents a believer. In Luke's account, the lost sheep stands for a person who comes to faith for the first time. And Jesus says, "There is more joy in heaven over one lost sinner who repents and returns to God than over ninety-nine others who are righteous and haven't strayed away!" (Luke 15:7 NLT). Both versions of the story teach us that the Good Shepherd dearly loves *all* of His sheep, whether they have just come to faith or whether they return to Him after a long time of wandering away.

Jesus is in the business of searching for, finding, and rescuing lost sheep, regardless of how those sheep got lost. Wandering sheep? Yup. Ignorant sheep? Yes. Sheep who don't even have enough sense to know they're lost or don't understand that they are broken? Why, yes, thank you so much for reminding me of my own story. The kind of lost sheep you are just doesn't matter.

Have you wandered away? Have you been distracted? Disobedient? Have you chosen to go your own way, even though you knew better? None of that matters, so long as you choose to return. In His mercy and love, the Good Shepherd seeks you out and brings you back to His side. And you don't have to waste time trying to "clean yourself up" first.

May I recommend that you take your cue from a little dog named Mason?

On April 27, 2011, a devastating storm swept through Alabama, reducing the city of Tuscaloosa to rubble. Meteorologists estimated the tornado to be a mile wide—the second-deadliest twister in U.S. history, causing more than three hundred fatalities. Witnesses captured terrifying images on their cell phones and posted them on YouTube and Facebook. The storm picked up homes and tossed them around like paper cups; cars flew through the air like children's toys.

In the midst of the tragedy and devastation, reports trickled out of some amazing, even miraculous rescues—stories that encouraged those still searching for missing friends and family.

One story in particular tugged at people's heartstrings, the tale of a little girl who refused to stop looking for her dog, Mason, a two-year-old terrier mix. On the day of the tornado, Mason got sucked out of the family garage and disappeared into the whirlwind. The twister reduced the family's home to rubble, but part of the porch remained standing. Day after day, family members returned to the devastated site in case their little dog had somehow, against all odds, survived the storm and found his way home.

Can you imagine their joy and surprise when a full *three weeks* after the storm hit they found Mason sitting on what remained of the front steps? No one knows how far he had to crawl on his two broken legs just to get there. His shattered bones looked ready to pierce his skin. Mason suffered from severe dehydration and had dropped to half his normal weight. But he was alive! And he had grimly determined to get home to the people who loved him. When he saw his family at last, this poor, miserable, terrible-looking little dog eagerly wagged his tail and hobbled toward them.[5]

It seems to me that we could learn a thing or two from this precious puppy. It didn't matter to him that he looked a mess. He felt no shame or embarrassment about his condition. He didn't try to run or hide or clean himself up to make himself more presentable.

He knew he was lost.

He knew his little world had been turned upside down.

He knew he needed help. And so he dragged himself home, straight into the arms of the ones who loved him.

Why is it that, so often, when we are bruised and broken, when we are a mess, we run *away* from the One who loves us? We hang our heads in shame and hope our presence will go unnoticed. We try to "fix" things on our own.

Maybe it's because we despise our brokenness. We feel ashamed of it and disgusted by it—and we think God must feel the same way. We don't understand how He could love us like He does. We can't quite believe it's true.

Somehow we must come to a place where we know in the deepest part of our souls that no matter what has happened to us, no matter how we have messed up, no matter how poor our choices, no matter how much we've failed or fallen short, God holds His arms wide open to receive us with boundless joy. He longs to welcome us safely home!

Some people who teach on the "lost sheep" passage almost make a joke about the shepherd being crazy enough to leave ninety-nine sheep in danger in order to go in search of one.

But that's no joke. That's the whole point.

God loves you *extravagantly*, and He will go to nearly any lengths to bring you back into the comfort of His arms and the safety of His flock.

(Of course, unlike any earthly shepherd, He's all-present and all-powerful. He can search for His lost lamb and still remain with the other ninety-nine!)

And when your Shepherd finds you, He doesn't scold you or ask you why you left. He doesn't demand His "pound of flesh." He doesn't say, "Okay, sheep, this is your last chance. One more trip off the radar and I'm done with you!" No, He carries you home on His shoulders and throws a party *because you are home!* That is the limitless grace and love of God extended to *every* lost lamb, however they wound up lost.

Does that sound unfair? I hope so, because it is. Grace isn't about "fair," but about the outrageous, radical love of God. And the reality is that—whether we see it or not—every one of us is or was that lost sheep.

White sheep.

Black sheep.

Crimson sheep.

It just doesn't matter.

Aren't we grateful that He came after *us*? Rejoiced over *us*, in the very same way? So why is it that sometimes we seem to make it harder for other lost sheep to come home?

What a Hussy!

I wonder if the ninety-nine sheep left behind patted each other on their woolly little backs for being such good, well-behaved sheep. I can hear the kinds of things they might have said about the lost sheep.

"There she goes again, wandering off—what a little hussy! I don't know why he wastes his time with her!"

"Oh, I quite agree, Marge. I asked her to help spread the grain out for the Wednesday night meeting last week, but she never showed up."

"And frankly, Trudy, between you and me, I think her wool is a bit short for a sheep of her age!"

"Took the words right out of my mouth, Marge!"

One time a woman labeled a "known sinner" crashed a private party to express her thanks to Jesus for caring about her. What a reputation to have in a small town! We don't know how she first encountered Christ or when she heard His message, believed in Him, and received His love. Perhaps she was one of the "multitudes" who listened to Him preach out in the fields or in the city streets. We do know that what Christ did for her so deeply moved her that all she wanted to do was say thank you personally and in a meaningful way.

She took a huge risk even showing up at the house of Simon the Pharisee—but what choice did she have? That's where Jesus was (see Luke 7).

This uninvited (and mostly unwelcome) guest knelt at Jesus' feet, weeping spontaneous tears of gratitude—a seemingly endless fountain—and wiping them with her hair. Everyone in the room began to point and whisper. How disturbing! Simon, the host, felt disgusted. But Jesus turned to him and served up his hypocrisy on a platter:

> "Do you see this woman? I entered your house; you gave me no water for my feet, but she has wet my feet with her tears and wiped them with her hair. You gave me no kiss, but from the time I came in she has not ceased to kiss my feet. You did not anoint my head with oil, but she has anointed my feet with ointment. Therefore I tell you, her sins, which are many, are forgiven—for she loved much. But he who is forgiven little, loves little."
> (Luke 7:44–47 ESV)

Jesus didn't mean that Simon hadn't sinned as much as this woman; only that Simon didn't see himself that way. Sometimes our own self-righteousness blinds us! And God, in His mercy, will do whatever it takes to open our eyes. He'll allow us to wander far enough to realize how lost we truly are—and always were.

I find it remarkable that this "known sinner" braved the insults, glares, snide comments, and rejection that surely she knew would fly. Unlike her, most of us wouldn't dare. Why risk it? Better to hunker down, put on some armor, build a few walls. Better to let no one get too close. Better to avoid any possibility of human connection . . . even if it means dying inside.

I know of some severely abused women who hurt so profoundly that they have told me, "I don't ever want to be vulnerable again." They mean by that, "I will never again let anyone get close enough to hurt me." And so they skim along on the surface of life, occasionally, perhaps, exchanging furtive glances with other men and women, but never touching down long enough to really connect. C. S. Lewis clearly had met such individuals himself, for he once wrote, "To love at all is to be vulnerable. Love anything, and your heart will certainly be wrung and possibly be broken. If you want to make sure of keeping it intact, you must give your heart to no one, not even to an animal . . . lock it up safe in the casket or coffin of your selfishness. But in that casket—safe, dark, motionless, airless—it will change. It will not be broken; it will become unbreakable, impenetrable, irredeemable."[6] Beth Moore said nearly the same thing in another way:

> Life's way of reacting to a crushed heart is to wrap tough sinews of flesh around it and tempt us to promise we'll never let ourselves get hurt again. That's not God's way. Remember, self-made fortresses not only keep love from going out; they keep love from coming in. We risk becoming captives in our own protective fortresses. Only God can put the pieces of our hearts back together again, close up all the wounds, and bind them with a porous bandage that protects from infection . . . but keeps the heart free to inhale and exhale love.[7]

I've said it before, and I'll say it again. Brokenness is a gift. Only sheep who know that they are broken—and yet loved—can learn to trust not in themselves but in the wisdom and strength and mercy and grace of the Good Shepherd.

THREE

OLD WOUNDS HAVE GOOD MEMORIES

Finding a Way Out of the Darkness

In the middle of the day, the sky grew as dark as night.

Not just black, like night. I recall shades of a deep, dark, military green that looked and felt *wrong*. The ominous color of the sky prompted cars to pull over to the side of the road, drivers wondering what to do.

I remember the incident as if it had happened only yesterday. Before the rain began pouring down in torrents and the lightning sent everyone scrambling for shelter, an eerie calm pervaded the whole fearsome scene. Even the birds seemed to stop moving, perched on branches as if waiting for something.

I parked behind two other cars under a bridge and turned off my engine. The driver in front of me ran back toward my car and knocked on the glass. I rolled down the window.

"I think we should get out of here," he said. "This looks like a twister!"

"It doesn't matter," I replied, without making eye contact.

I couldn't see how he reacted to my words, but I watched him run back to his car, grab his briefcase, and disappear from sight.

I sat there with tears streaming down my face. I couldn't stop repeating, "I'm sorry. I am so, so sorry!"

As crazy as it sounds, I believed deep in my heart that this storm was *my* fault, that all of heaven had united in a rage against me. A big part of that misbelief came from a desperate lack of understanding about the true nature of God and His fierce love for me.

Seeing but Not Understanding

As I sat weeping in the car that day, certain that my actions had brought on the wrath of God, I felt like a lost, lonely stray—a wicked, wandering, religious vagrant with nowhere to run and nowhere to call home.

Under a bridge in the dark seemed like a logical place to be.

These moments are shocking. I never wanted to be a stray, lost and alone in a dark place. I've always wanted to be strong. I've always wanted to be the one collecting strays and helping them find their feet. I saw my own brokenness as weakness, and weakness terrified me. To be weak is to be vulnerable.

I now know, of course, that those fears got etched into my very soul as a little girl. Old wounds have disgustingly good memories, but abysmally poor interpretive skills. While the pain keeps the memory fresh and alive (at least, like a zombie is alive), it also obscures the truth and keeps you from accurately understanding what really happened. The closest analogy I can think of is the way children tend to hear and see everything around them, but fail to comprehend much of it.

It used to amaze me that my son, Christian, could sit in the backseat of our car, seemingly engrossed in a game, and just moments after I would say something very quietly to Barry, a little voice would pipe up: "I don't think that's how it was, Mom."

How did he hear that? I wondered.

Children seem to see and hear everything—but often incorrectly interpret that information. They draw the wrong conclusions. When their parents' marriage ends, for example, inevitably they internalize and personalize what happened.

Would Dad have stayed if I'd kept my room cleaner?

Did Mom leave because I didn't help around the house?

What could I have done? What did I do?

It must have been my fault.

My father died when I was just five years old. I'd always been a "daddy's girl," but when he suffered a cerebral hemorrhage in 1961, he became partially paralyzed and eventually unable to speak. I clung to him as his interpreter—but soon his personality began to change, growing dark and violent. One day, alerted by my dog's growl, I just averted a blow to my head from my father's cane. He threw my mother against a wall, and it took four men to subdue him and take him to a psychiatric hospital. Sometime later he escaped, and they found his body in the river. He was just thirty-four years old.

For me, my father's violence, even though caused by a brain injury, indicated that he saw something so bad in me that he wanted to end my life. The very last time he looked in my eyes, I saw nothing but pure hatred.

I loved my dad, and in my young mind, he could not have been wrong—which meant something really terrible *had* to be in me. After he died, I determined that no one would ever again get close enough to me to see what my dad saw.

This deadly strategy spilled over into my relationship with God. I determined to be the perfect Christian woman so that God would never see anything in me that might make Him turn from me in disgust or stop loving me.

How could I bear to ever see "that look" in *His* eyes?

A dark path? Yes, it was. But it's a path that many walk to this day.

What Is Wrong with Me?

I receive hundreds of notes every year from women all around the world who struggle with a similarly distorted image of themselves, usually because of things that happened in their past. Certain themes repeat themselves endlessly:

- "My dad didn't just leave my mom; he left me too. What did I do wrong?"
- "My father had no time for me as a little girl. Now I just try and blend into the background."
- "My mother told me I was stupid. She was right. I mess up everything."
- "My husband is abusive, but I deserve it."
- "When I look in the mirror, all I see is a fat, unlovable woman."
- "I'll always be single. Who would want to marry me?"
- "I can't have children. I think God is punishing me for things I've done in the past."

While the list never stops growing, the theme always remains the same: "What is *wrong* with me?" Without a doubt, old wounds really do have good memories! Sometimes, in fact, those old images are so potent that they begin to turn us physically into the thing that we dwell on mentally.

I remember a woman I worked for one summer as a teenager. I knew her a little as someone who had attended our church, but until she became my boss for those few months, I had kept my distance from her. She always seemed so stern and disapproving. Her countenance resounded a gigantic "No!" before you ever asked a question.

My heart sank when I realized I would have to report to her each morning. But as the mornings turned to weeks and to months, my heart for this woman changed, and I looked for ways to serve her. I watched her hands, bent and twisted with arthritis, struggle to pick up a pencil or hold a cup. I listened as she talked about her bitterly disappointing life. As she allowed stories of one rejection after another, years of serving ill parents with little thanks, to spill out, it seemed to me that the exterior of her body mirrored the interior of her spirit. It seemed as though she never had managed to gladly give, that everything had been taken or snatched from her, which left her bitter and twisted both inside and out. She wore this graceless life like a heavy overcoat of shame.

Guilt and Shame

In his wonderful book *Shame and Grace*, Lewis Smedes wrote, "The difference between guilt and shame is very clear—in theory. We feel guilty for what we do. We feel shame for what we are."[8]

I'll never forget the moment I first read that statement. I wanted to shout, "That's *it*! That's *exactly* what I've been feeling but couldn't find words for." Grasping this idea was huge for me, like finding a key to a dark cellar that I'd feared to enter because of what I might find.

Think of it this way: If you have *done* something wrong, then you can try to put it right. You can ask for forgiveness and seek to make restitution. But if at the depth of your soul you believe that you *are* something wrong, then what can you do with *that*?

No Seraphim Here

Before we go further, I need to make an important distinction. Most of the time when people these days talk about shame, they speak of it as a universally bad thing, as something to be shunned and avoided. We get the impression that if we could just do away with shame, through whatever means necessary, we'd all be a lot better off.

As someone who over the years has suffered greatly from shame, I have to admit that my heart loves the idea of sending it far, far away—or maybe blasting it off the face of the planet. But then I read the Bible, and it seems to tell me, "Not so fast, Sheila."

The Bible uses a lot of words, in both Hebrew and Greek, to describe various aspects of what we call "shame." In general, the Bible sees shame as "a condition of humiliating disgrace."[9] In a large number of passages, people like King David say to God, "Do not let me be put to shame" (Psalm 25:2), or on the flip side, "Let the wicked be put to shame" (Psalm 31:17). Nobody *likes* to feel shame; no one *wants* to feel humiliated and disgraced. I don't, and I doubt you do either. And the glorious promise of the gospel is that those who place their faith in Christ will ultimately be delivered forever from shame and its shadow.

Several times the New Testament, taking its cue from the Old Testament, declares that those who put their trust in God "will never be put to shame" (Romans 9:33; see also Romans 10:11; 1 Peter 2:6; Psalm 25:3). When one day in heaven we stand before God, clothed in the brilliant righteousness of Christ, we will never feel shame again. Hallelujah!

Okay, but just take a quick look around you. See any seraphim? How about pearly gates? No, I don't see them either, and there's a simple explanation for that.

We're not home yet.

On this fallen planet, *some* shame apparently still has work to do—and unless I'm badly mistaken, divinely appointed work. We have Adam and Eve to thank for that.

Before Adam and Eve disobeyed God in the garden of Eden, shame had no place in their hearts. So the Bible says that the "man and his wife were both naked, and they felt no shame" (Genesis 2:25). Why would they? They enjoyed perfect, free, and unstained relationships with God and each other. No secrets. No jealousy. Nothing to hide. Nothing to regret. Before sin entered Eden, shame could no more grow there than a banana tree could grow on the dark side of the moon.

Sin, of course, changed everything. Once Adam and Eve disobeyed God, shame found the ideal conditions for growth inside their freshly fallen hearts, like noxious weeds sprouting in an untended greenhouse. We've been trying to eradicate those weeds ever since.

We wilt under the load of shame. It didn't exist in human hearts before the Fall. God has banned it from heaven, eternally. So shame is a bad thing, right?

Well, maybe not altogether.

You see, I keep bumping into verses such as Psalm 83:16, where Asaph makes a startling request of God regarding some people he considered his enemies. "Cover their faces with shame," he wrote, which I might have expected; but then he continued, *"so that men will seek your name*, O LORD" (emphasis added). I didn't see that one coming. Did you?

It seems that in a world mortally wounded by disobedience and fatally infected with the disease of sin, shame has a role to play in God's redemptive purposes. God intends to use *even shame* to bring us to Himself, where we can live free of shame forever.

In case you hoped this might be only an Old Testament strategy, allow me to draw your attention to four verses from a book in the New Testament. I found them all very enlightening, if quite surprising.

The apostle Paul, often called "the apostle of grace," had a tough time with one of the churches he helped to found. The Corinthian congregation always seemed to go off the rails, whether in conduct or doctrine. So Paul wrote 1 Corinthians, hoping to get them back on track. In the very first chapter of his letter, he wrote, "God chose the foolish things of the world to shame the wise; God chose the weak things of the world to shame the strong" (1:27). The Greek term translated "shame" means "put to shame, be humiliated."

Oh, and notice who's doing the shaming here.

It's God Himself.

Our gracious Lord—who loves us enough to have sent His only Son into the world to die for our sins so that we might live forever with Him—sometimes uses shame to bring people to Himself.

Of course, God doesn't use shame always, or even frequently, and certainly not randomly. And neither do His servants. So Paul, a little later in his letter, said, "I am not writing this to shame you, but to warn you, as my dear children" (4:14). The Greek word translated "shame" here differs from the term found in 1 Corinthians 1:27, but not by much. It means "to make someone ashamed." At this point in his letter, Paul didn't want to use shame to motivate a godly change in his friends; he hoped a simple warning would do the trick.

Two chapters later, however, the apostle changed his tone. He could hardly believe that some members of this church had decided to take fellow church members to court over arguments about money. You can almost hear him saying, "Are you kidding me? Seriously? You would do this? You would drag fellow Christians into court in front of pagan judges? I can't believe this! What are you thinking?"

Why in the world, he wondered, couldn't they find mediators in their own church body? "Isn't there anyone in all the church who is wise enough to decide these issues?" (6:5 NLT).

What's going on here? This doesn't sound like the kind and gentle Paul of a few chapters before. He even wrote, "I say this to shame you" (6:5), using the same term employed in 1 Corinthians 4:14 (when he said he *didn't* want to shame them). So here was Paul, the great apostle, writing under the inspiration of the Holy Spirit, who deliberately used shame as a wake-up call to some believers who weren't thinking very clearly.

But he wasn't done yet.

Toward the end of his letter, after calling out all sorts of sins and foolish behavior of this church, he let loose with one last volley:

Come back to your senses as you ought, and stop sinning; for there are some who are ignorant of God—I say this to your shame. (15:34)

The term translated "shame" in this verse is the same one the apostle used in the previous two instances. Paul saw it as shameful—and even more, he wanted the Corinthians to *feel* this shame—that the church had become so lax that it included some individuals in its membership who didn't even believe in the resurrection of Christ from the dead. These unbelieving people Paul called "ignorant of God."

But don't miss his zinger in 15:34: "I say this to your shame."

He intended it as a fleeting tactic to prompt his friends—true Christians, not unbelievers—to come back to their senses.

I don't like shame, or any part of it. I don't like the way it makes me feel. But apparently sometimes—*sometimes*—shame can be a tool in the hands of the Holy Spirit to bring us into fellowship with Himself, either for the first time or even after we have known Him for some time.

Shame as Cholesterol

I think shame has a lot in common with cholesterol. Cholesterol is a "fat steroid" produced in our liver or intestines that the body uses to manufacture vitamin D, certain hormones, and other chemicals required for building healthy cell membranes. We can't do without it, and our blood carries it throughout our body.

Doctors tell us, however, that we have both "good" and "bad" cholesterol. Good cholesterol—HDL, or high-density lipoproteins—keeps us healthy by protecting our cardiovascular system. Bad cholesterol—LDL, or low-density lipoproteins—tends to do nasty things like clog our arteries, paving the way for heart attacks. Unfortunately, most of the cholesterol in our modern bodies tends to be of the LDL variety, in many cases because we eat too many fatty foods.

So why do I think cholesterol and shame have a lot in common?

For two reasons. First, because it comes into our lives in two forms: good and bad. And second, because the bad tends to outnumber and overwhelm the good.

So many of the women I speak to around the country come to me with shame weighing down their weary bodies. They live with shame (if you can call it living), and it beats them down lower than earthworms. In the vast number of cases, these women are living with LDL shame (lying, demonic language). Somewhere in their past, a trusted friend, family member, or authority figure took a flamethrower to their self-esteem—"You're no good, and you'll always be no good," "Why can't you do anything right?" "You're so stupid, you'll fail at anything you try"—and they keep mentally replaying these lies, over and over again, endlessly.

So long as they allow the LDL to accumulate in their systems, they become more and more at risk for a spiritual (or even physical) heart attack. As my friend Dr. Henry Cloud explained to me, when we dwell in these LDLs, the three Ps kick in: Personal, Pervasive, and Permanent.

Personal—we think everything that's going wrong in our lives is our fault.

Pervasive—we think the trouble is not just in us but it's all around us too.

Permanent—we think our lives will never change; it will always be this way.

A few of the people I have met talk to me about some persistent sin in their lives, but they want to know how to get rid of the shame, not the sin. In them, I sense HDL shame at work (holy-discipline language). God is attempting to use this "good" shame to grab their attention, get them to think and go in a new direction. He never uses a lot of it, just enough to bring spiritual health.

A friend of mine told me that, many years ago, he heard Bishop George McKinney of St. Stephen's Cathedral Church of God in Christ give a sermon on Christian living. As my friend remembers it, Bishop McKinney thundered, "People today don't want to know how to live holy. People today want to know how to fornicate safely."

Because we all suffer from the sort of debased desires that Bishop McKinney so colorfully lamented, God in His mercy has created HDL shame. Without it, we can end up on the wrong side of some frightening verses: "Are they ashamed of their loathsome conduct? No, they have no shame at all; they do not even know how to blush" (Jeremiah 6:15; see also Jeremiah 3:3; 8:12).

Although I do not *like* the way shame feels, today I can thank God for creating the HDL variety. I know, however, that most of the shame I encounter in women today is the bad version . . . the artery-clogging, heart-destroying, lying, demonic kind.

So the question becomes, "How do I get rid of LDL shame? How do I stop listening to the satanic lies and start living by health-promoting truth?"

While in this book I can't give you a fully developed how-to plan on how to change your thinking—whole books have been written profitably on the subject (I think of William Backus's work in *Telling Yourself the Truth*, for example)—I believe I can point you in the right direction.

Time to Take Action

One of the great challenges of our brokenness is training our hearts to hear God's love above the din of our LDL shame. The *only* way I know of doing that is by changing our thinking, a process that usually takes a long time and requires innumerable skirmishes against the enemy of our souls, who wants to keep us in darkness and in pain.

You *can* win this battle, though. I know you can, because I've met countless women who are doing exactly that, and I'm learning to do so myself. To help you get started on the right path, I'd like to give you three action steps. Not enough, perhaps, for you to obliterate the enemy and declare victory, but enough to begin turning the tide of war.

And even that much is wonderful.

By the way, it *is* a war. I hope that in all the "dailyness" of life you never forget that! You are in a spiritual battle that will last the rest of your life. Your enemy, the devil, prowls the earth like a ravenous lion, seeking someone to devour. It may even be that he's been chewing on *you*. If so, it's past time to get his teeth out of you by sinking your own teeth into the Word of God.

I said earlier that old wounds have good memories. But that's really only half the story. It's *also* a fact that God's truth trumps even the strongest of those memories. If you want to change your thinking, you have to renew your mind—and that takes work. I encourage you to start that process by focusing on the following three critical strategies.

1. *Talking to yourself is normal. Just make sure that you say the right things.*

This first strategy does not come from pop psychology, but from Scripture itself. Listen to the psalmist:

> *Why are you downcast, O my soul?*
> *Why so disturbed within me?*
> *Put your hope in God,*
> > *for I will yet praise him,*
> > *my Savior and my God.*

(PSALM 42:5–6)

We all talk to ourselves. We do it in a thousand ways and often without realizing it. The point is to tell ourselves the truth, rather than carelessly echo the false and hurtful lies of our enemy. The first step toward renewing your mind is to recognize that you really do speak to your own soul. So make up your mind to speak only true words!

2. Fill your mind with the truth of God's Word.

I strongly recommend that you build an arsenal of Scripture verses tucked into your mind, ready for use at all times. If you have never made Scripture memory a practice, focus on two key things as you begin:

The first is to dwell on *who God says He is (and who He is for you)*.

You need to build an arsenal particular to you and specific to your challenges and needs. Still, let me give you a few passages that have proven especially meaningful to me:

- "The LORD is my light and my salvation; whom shall I fear? The LORD is the stronghold of my life; of whom shall I be afraid?" (Psalm 27:1 ESV).
- "Let the morning bring me word of your unfailing love, for I have put my trust in you. Show me the way I should go, for to you I lift up my soul" (Psalm 143:8).
- "For I am convinced that neither death nor life, neither angels nor demons, neither the present nor the future, nor any powers, neither height nor depth, nor anything else in all creation, will be able to separate us from the love of God that is in Christ Jesus our Lord" (Romans 8:38–39).
- "He who dwells in the shelter of the Most High will rest in the shadow of the Almighty. I will say of the LORD, 'He is my refuge and my fortress, my God, in whom I trust'" (Psalm 91:1).

Second, take a hard look at *who God says you are (and what you are to Him)*.

Once you have a clearer understanding of the true nature of God, you need to fortify yourself with a clearer understanding of your new nature in Christ. Again, the verses you choose should speak strongly to your own soul. But in case you'd like a few potent examples, let me list some texts that have really helped me:

- "I can do all things through him who strengthens me" (Philippians 4:13 ESV).
- "There is therefore now no condemnation for those who are in Christ Jesus" (Romans 8:1 ESV).
- "You did not choose me, but I chose you and appointed you that you should go and bear fruit and that your fruit should abide, so that whatever you ask the Father in my name, he may give it to you" (John 15:16 ESV).

· "But he said to me, 'My grace is sufficient for you, for my power is made
perfect in weakness.' Therefore I will boast all the more gladly of my
weaknesses, so that the power of Christ may rest upon me" (2 Corinthians
12:9 ESV).

Evangelist Luis Palau has helped hundreds of thousands of people come
to faith in Christ worldwide, and one text that he uses frequently comes
from the book of Hebrews. So many hurting people approach him, feeling
overwhelmed with guilt and wracked with shame. They hear the gospel, but
they simply can't believe it could apply to *them*. A woman named Sue called
Luis one evening on a live television show he often hosts in the middle of
one of his evangelistic outreaches. She sobbed that she had slept with a
married coworker, a longtime family friend. "I know I broke one of God's
laws," she wept. "I know that God would never, ever forgive me for this."

"I want to contradict you," Luis replied. "God *will* forgive you."

But Sue couldn't believe it. The guilt and shame she felt for betraying
her husband simply overpowered her. "I failed God," she kept repeating. "I
just don't know what to do. I'm devastated."

Luis finally quoted for Sue the promise of Hebrews 9:14, which says,
"The blood of Christ, who through the eternal Spirit offered himself
unblemished to God, will cleanse our consciences from acts that lead to
death, so that we may serve the living God!"

"That's fine," Sue answered, "but I just don't feel cleansed."

Luis explained that God remains faithful even when we don't, and then
he asked, "Sue, do you want to be forgiven, or do you want to wallow in misery for the rest of your life?"

"No," she replied, "I want to be forgiven!"

And then Luis got to the heart of the matter—for Sue, and for all of us,
regardless of the sins we have committed:

How do you settle adultery right? You confess your sin. You accept the for-
giveness of God. Don't go through this baloney of "I can't forgive myself."
No, you can't forgive yourself. No one can. God forgives us, and we accept
His forgiveness and we are forgiven. God will say to you from His Word,
"Woman, I forgive you because I died in your place for that dirty little sin."
From then on you are free, as though you had never committed that sin.

The Lord will forgive you and cleanse you, and you can walk in freedom.
You will be free in Christ to walk with God.

Luis reported, "Sue finally understood, and by the end of our conversation she had found release from the guilt that had been crushing her."[10]

If you feel crushed beneath the weight of guilt and shame, the same
truth applies to you, and in the same way. Believe what God says about you—
that when you confess your sin, turn from it, and ask God to cleanse you, He
will—and begin to live in freedom.

3. *Surround yourself with loving, godly people who will remind you of the truth.*

God didn't design the Christian life to be lived in isolation. In fact, it's
quite the opposite. Sitting cross-legged by yourself in a black robe in the
back of some Middle Eastern cave might sound healthy and holy to some,
but you won't find that manner of life promoted in Scripture.

The simple fact is you need others, and they need you. You need to hear
their words of blessing, affection, and encouragement, and they need to
hear yours. Never underestimate the power of the words that others speak
into your life, whether for good or for ill! Proverbs 18:21 declares, "The
tongue has the power of life and death." Positive, true, affirming words can
literally turn a life around.

Howard grew up in a broken home. His parents divorced right after his
birth—he always thought he'd caused the split—and his grandmother reared
him. He spent most of his elementary school years as a self-described
troublemaker, a hell-raiser, in a poor neighborhood of Philadelphia. His
fifth-grade teacher, Miss Simon, once tied Howard to his seat with a rope
and taped his mouth shut. She predicted that five boys in her class would
end up in prison, Howard among them. She was right about three of them.

Howard has no good memories of the fifth grade.

The following year, when Howard introduced himself to his sixth-grade
teacher, Miss Noe said something that would change his life forever. "I've
heard a lot about you," she said, prompting Howard to think, *Here we go
again*. But then she continued with a gentle, encouraging smile, "But I don't
believe a word of it."

From that moment forward, Miss Noe made Howard realize *for the first time in his life* that someone cared. "People are always looking for someone to say, 'Hey, I believe in you,'" Howard says today.[11]

By the way, Howard's last name is Hendricks. As a celebrated professor at Dallas Seminary for more than half a century, he has taught, inspired, and mentored many of America's most gifted Bible teachers, including Chuck Swindoll, David Jeremiah, Tony Evans, Bruce Wilkinson, and scores of others.

Surround yourself with people who will speak the truth, in love, to your soul. And let that truth transform your mind and renew your life.

From Helplessness to Hope

As a young man, my husband's grandfather became the victim of a violent robbery. Thieves broke into the grocery store where he worked, beat him, nailed him into a large whiskey barrel, and left him to die. The following day coworkers discovered him . . . alive but profoundly changed.

For the rest of his life, this man lived in fear, tormented by the voices of the robbers in his head and by the dank, dismal darkness of the barrel he felt sure would become his casket. His fear was palpable and personal, but also pervasive, and it found its way deep into the heart of his son, William— the father of my husband, Barry.

Barry's first memory of how that fear affected him occurred as he watched the news one night with his dad when Barry was about five years old. A young local boy had drowned in a boating accident, and as William let the story drape him in dread, he said to Barry, "You are *never* to get in a boat. That's what will happen to you if you are ever out on the water." Barry remembers fear gripping his heart as he imagined what it would feel like to struggle for air, helpless, with no hope at all. As he grew up, he learned to hide his fear; but every now and then, it would betray him.

When Barry and I first got married, I dropped a Christmas ornament that read, "Our first Christmas 1994." He turned to me with a stricken look on his face and said, "What do you think that means?"

I told him, "I think it means . . . you married a klutz!"

"No," he continued, "I mean, do you think that is a sign?"

"Yes," I replied, "I think it may mean you're a nutcase!"

He smiled, but I saw something deeper in his eyes. As Christmas 1996 approached, Barry and I prepared to welcome our son into the world. "I want this to stop here and now," Barry said to me one night. "I want the legacy of lies and fear and helplessness to end with me. I will *not* pass this on to our son."

I have watched as Barry intentionally replaced the lies that had been his legacy with the life-giving words of Scripture. He memorized many scriptures, and every night he prayed a powerful prayer excerpted from Richard Foster's book, *Prayer*:

> By the authority of almighty God, I tear down Satan's strongholds in my life, in the lives of those I love, and in the society in which I live. I take into myself the weapons of truth, righteousness, salvation, the word of God, and prayer. I command every evil influence to leave; you have no right here and I allow you no point of entry. I ask for an increase of faith, hope, and love so that, by the power of God, I can be a light set on a hill, causing truth and justice to flourish. These things I pray for the sake of him who loved me and gave himself for me. Amen.[12]

I watch Barry now fishing from a boat with our son, and I think that although old wounds have good memories, no nightmare is a match for our Savior's redemptive love. As you reflect on your life and the places where shame has clothed you, would you be willing to bring the lies, the fear, and the darkness to Christ? Shame tells us that our brokenness is forever. The cross of Jesus Christ tells us that He took the forever of brokenness on Himself so that we can live, forever, in freedom.

FOUR

RELENTLESS QUESTIONS

His Presence and Peace in Your Darkest Nights and Longest Battles

Before she said a word, she held out her hand. I saw the red rubber bracelet she offered, hoping I would take it and wear it. At that moment, I didn't yet know the story behind that bracelet; I just knew that it had one.

In a box at home I have fifteen such bracelets, each engraved with the name of a child. Most have a favorite scripture.

The saddest ones have a date.

These simple bracelets, fashioned out of hard rubber, have become common currency in our culture. I think the first one I became aware of belonged to Lance Armstrong. His yellow Nike band—"Just do it!"—brought international attention to his fight against the ghastly beast of cancer.

But the bands aren't really about celebrities or famous people with famous causes. My son ordered thirty rubber bracelets in black, emblazoned with his favorite scripture: "My grace is sufficient for you, for my power is made perfect in weakness" (2 Corinthians 12:9). He gave one to each of his school friends . . . a much-needed reminder in high school.

I was given one once by a disturbingly enthusiastic woman. It reads, "Lose weight now, ask me how!" I gave that one a decent Christian burial in the trash can.

I wear two such bracelets every day. One reminds me to pray for the Suffering Church around the world, for those who share my faith but not my freedom. It says simply, "One With Them." The other I wear in support of the "A21 campaign," which battles to free human beings sold into sex slavery. But each of the fifteen bracelets I have in my box at home tells a very particular, very individual story.

I took the red rubber bracelet the women held out to me and slipped it on my wrist. "It's to remember my son," she explained. "He died when he was the age your boy is now." I thanked her for sharing this holy gift with me, and as she allowed herself to sink into my arms for just a moment, I felt as if she bore the weight of the world on her very fragile shoulders. But like so many women I have met who have walked through the unbearable pain of losing a child, she has fought to find the strength to go on for those who still need her.

Finally she stood up, pulled herself together, and walked away. As she disappeared from sight, I prayed for hope and comfort and grace, asking God to wrap His arms around her and shelter her on those nights, sure to come, when her strength dries up and only the questions remain.

Questions, Questions, and the Question

Not all fifteen of my rubber bracelets bear the finality of dates like this one did. Some have the name of a child in a very present battle with cancer; but every one of them reminds me of the relentless questions that remain unanswered for so many.

One band has only two words on it, the name of a daughter and the question, "Why?"

For as far back as we have walked on this planet as sons of Adam and daughters of Eve, we have asked the *why* questions. One of the earliest instances in the Bible was with Rebekah, the wife of Isaac, who went to ask the Lord about the two babies who were jostling one another in her womb. Something didn't feel right; it troubled her, so she asked the Lord, "Why is this happening to me?" (Genesis 25:22).

In that instance, the Lord gave a detailed answer, not only about the current circumstance, but how it would play out over the years to come.

But He usually doesn't do that.

There are many times when God declines to answer our *why* questions, whispering, *"Trust Me,"* instead. But that doesn't always satisfy us, does it? When the answers we long for don't come, we ask and we ask and we ask because everything inside us rages that life was never supposed to be this way.

Why, God?
Why am I here?
Does my life have any purpose?
Do You hear my prayers?

Why do You ask me to pray if You already know what You are going to do?

Why did her child get healed and mine died?

Was it my fault?

Should I have had more faith?

Why didn't You save my marriage?

What more could I have done?

Why didn't You stop me from playing the fool?

Are You angry with me?

Are You disappointed in me?

Do You love me?

But I hear one question more than any other, over and over again: *"Why do children suffer?"* That one packs the biggest punch of all, for it takes the very breath from countless numbers who feel sentenced to watch and endure, while unable to make the pain go away.

Imagine that you are a pastor and that your beautiful little girl faces round after round of chemotherapy in a bloody battle to kill the cancerous tumor in her brain. How do you stand on a platform, week after week, and speak of a God who is both powerful and loving? That is what Aaron McRae has faced since Monday, June 29, 2009. He heard the news from a brief phone call with his wife, Holly.

Sweet Kate . . . and So It Begins

Holly explained the beginning of their ordeal in a brief, pain-filled note:

Monday June 29, 2009, was supposed to be a day filled with summer fun. The kids and I were going to the water park to celebrate summer. However, I noticed that a slight tremor in Kate's right hand had developed over the past few days had notably worsened. We decided to take her to her pediatrician, just for safe measure. A CT of Kate's head was ordered. We proceeded to Phoenix Children's Hospital for a stat CT of her head. At 5:30 I, Holly, Kate's mom, was taken into a room alone and told Kate had a massive tumor on the left temporal lobe of her brain. The world seemed to stop for us that day. I called her dad and through sobs told him to come to the hospital quickly.

No warning bells or neon signs prepare you for this kind of awful, life-bending event. One moment, a water park; the next, words that never should be uttered: "Your five-year-old daughter has a massive tumor on her brain."

I first became aware of this family through Twitter, one of the most popular social networking sites these days. But in the months and years that followed, we have become good friends. I have visited Kate in the hospital in Phoenix (more about that visit later) and spent some time with Holly, Kate, and her sister, Olivia, here in Texas. Aaron and their son, Will, came to hear me speak one night in Phoenix.

Well, Aaron did. Will played "Angry Birds" on my iPad.

Endless Days

It became clear from the first surgery that Kate has a very aggressive form of cancer. To increase her chances of survival and to minimize long-term side effects, Kate was placed into an ongoing study. The path has not been easy.

The study involves the initial brain surgery, five rounds of intense chemotherapy with the possibility of a subsequent brain surgery, and then another round of chemo with a stem cell transplant.

As I write these words, Kate and her family are in the middle of it all. Kate is slated for yet another MRI to gauge the effectiveness of the treatment so far. The days have seemed endless:

2 years, 4 months, and 17 days

124 weeks

869 days

I have joined the band of prayer warriors who call out Kate's name at the throne of mercy as part of our daily lives. But for Aaron and Holly, this is their life. They don't get to walk away and forget for a while. Hour by hour, they stay vigilant about Kate's health while trying to remain the mom and dad that Olivia and Will need too.

As a mother, I particularly relate deeply to Holly's gut-wrenching pain.

But I know how Aaron suffers as well. Consider this recent note that he posted:

One of my favorite stories of Scripture is of the Roman captain who came to Jesus on behalf of his sick servant in Matthew 8. I love the reality that Jesus seems willing and even eager to heal this servant simply by saying, "I will go and heal him." I believe Jesus is God, He is Lord, and He is the Healer. This was absolutely true of Jesus a couple of thousand years ago, and it is still true today.

For me, the story becomes even more intriguing when Jesus, astounded and amazed, declares that He has never found such faith in any other person. This despised Roman soldier astonished Jesus. That's so incredible to me.

Reflecting on this story makes me ask a ton of questions: questions like . . . does Jesus still heal when we ask Him? Does Jesus desire to heal our Katie-bear? Do I have the kind of faith to "amaze" Jesus? If not, why not?

It's hard enough to watch your child suffer, but adding to that the load of "Is my faith amazing enough, and if not, why not?" seems too much to bear. Would God expect parents—broken and bent from wretched days and sleepless nights—to be able to produce anything "amazing"?

Nevertheless, Aaron is right. The faith of that long-ago Roman centurion "amazed" Jesus. It's one of only two times that Scripture describes Jesus as "amazed"—once at the faith of this man and once at the unbelief of the Jews:

> And Jesus said to them, "A prophet is not without honor, except in his hometown and among his relatives and in his own household." And he could do no mighty work there, except that he laid his hands on a few sick people and healed them. And he marveled because of their unbelief. (Mark 6:4–6 ESV)

It's funny, though. We take no comfort in the fact that most of the people didn't believe and didn't get it. We simply torment ourselves with the *one man* who did get it. And we wonder:

> *How did he get that kind of faith?*
> *What did he know that I don't?*
> *How can I amaze God?*

I have encountered that kind of torturous self-evaluation in many places. I got a letter from a terminally ill young woman, for example, who saw me pray on my knees one morning on television and decided that per-haps *that* was the key she was missing. *That* was why God wasn't answering her prayers; it all has to do with posture. So she got down on weak and frag-ile knees . . . and promptly dislocated her hipbone.

I wept when I read her letter.

Honestly, I did more than weep. I threw my Bible across my office. It wasn't that I was angry at God—I was angry over *what we have made of Him*. My anger and frustration center on some of the lies perpetrated in His name. I think here of the "prosperity" garbage peddled in the '80s and '90s that did so much damage to broken people. It mocks those who love God but for whom the formula of "If you have enough faith, you can name it and claim it" simply doesn't work.

The truth is, such a perverted doctrine doesn't work for *anyone*, no matter what people tell you.

God isn't some cosmic jukebox in the sky, from which, so long as you have the right coin, you get to pick the soundtrack for your life. Those who peddle a health-and-wealth message have wounded uncounted thousands who are left reeling with only one conclusion: *The reason that my child died, or that my mar-riage failed, or that we lost our house . . . is because I didn't have enough faith.*

That is beyond cruel; it is blasphemous.

Christ never promised an easy path. He never said there would be roses with no thorns, or seasons without winter, or pathways without obstacles. In fact, quite the opposite. Before He was arrested and forced into a mock-ery of a trial, Jesus told those closest to Him, "In this world you will have trouble. But take heart! I have overcome the world" (John 16:33).

There it is, a promise the prosperity preachers never put up on the TV screen:

> "YOU WILL HAVE TROUBLE."
> —Jesus Christ

No, He never promised us an easy road.

What Christ *does* promise, though, are His presence and His peace in the darkest nights and the longest battles.

As I bent over to pick up my Bible, a source of life and strength to millions through the ages and to me, I acknowledged again that my anger and frustration really focused on the chasm that seems to exist at times between a loving God and a broken world.

It was never supposed to be like this.

The Rage of Christ

My secretary popped her head into my office. She had heard the loud *thud* as my study Bible hit the wall.

"Okay, boss?" she asked with a grin.

I smiled back. "I'm all right . . . so is the wall. It just breaks my heart to see so much pain. How does God hold Himself back from intervening?"

She smiled and nodded in empathy and closed my office door behind her as she left.

That night I dug through my New Testament, looking for something I had read just a few days before but had rushed over. Apparently it got caught somewhere inside me, though, and I needed to make sure I remembered it right.

You can find the story in John 11. Apart from the resurrection of Christ, I find it the most profoundly moving story in the Gospels. A man named Lazarus, dead for four days, gets brought back to life. It becomes especially memorable for me because this man and his sisters, Martha and Mary, had become some of Jesus' closest friends. He had spent time at their house, where they talked, laughed, prayed, and dined on Martha's good cooking together. So when it became clear to the women that their brother, Lazarus, had grown gravely ill, they sent for Jesus to come quickly.

But He didn't.

Not the first day, and not the second either.

The message was sent, and the message was received. But Jesus stayed where He was. The text makes it clear that He *intentionally* didn't come in time. And Lazarus died. Only after His friend had died—when it was "too late"—did Jesus arrive. By that time, Lazarus had been buried, and the funeral flowers had all wilted.

The text makes the pain of the sisters palpable. Martha and Mary stand side by side with every other man, woman, or child down through the years who has watched someone they love suffer and begged God to show up on time . . . and He doesn't.

So when Jesus finally arrived, "Mary came to where Jesus was and saw him, she fell at his feet, saying to him, 'Lord, if you had been here, my brother would not have died'" (John 11:32 ESV). Can you hear the pain in her voice? "Why? Why didn't You come when we needed You here? Why, Lord, why? You could have done this! You could have saved him! Why?"

Martha asked the same questions, in a nearly identical way. So we know the sisters had talked about their mutual confusion and pain. "Where were You, Lord? Why?" But it's not their questions that amaze me. They *should* have asked! We all want to know, "If You are big enough to stop it, Lord, then why don't You? Where were You when we needed You?" No, I didn't return to the text to search for what Mary or Martha *asked*.

I wanted to remind myself of what Jesus *felt*:

> When Jesus saw her weeping, and the Jews who had come with her also weeping, he was deeply *moved* in his spirit and greatly troubled. (John 11:33 ESV, emphasis added)

The English translation doesn't do justice to the weight of what Christ felt. The Greek term translated "moved" is *embrimaomai*. It's a strong word denoting anger, strength, or the bellowing and snorting of a horse. In other words, as Christ looked at the grief of His friends, He felt a rage, a fury at what sin has done to this world.

"Moved"?

No . . . that doesn't even come close.

I feel "moved" when my son tells me he loves me, or my dog rests her head on my lap. But what Jesus experienced went far beyond some sentimental, warm feeling; far from it! This was the Son of God raging at the pain that Mary and Martha, that Aaron and Holly, that you and I have faced or are facing right now.

I love that! It deeply comforts me that rather than gloss over our pain and casually point to the promise of heaven, Christ rages with us. John tells us, too, that Christ wept.

All this reassures me that we don't follow a Lord immune to our suffering. Christ feels our pain deeply.

But I see a *huge* question tucked just under the covers of that comfort. If Christ hates it so much, then why doesn't He just stop it?

Pick One!

That was the bottom-line question for a woman with whom I once spent some time. Already she had buried two children. She simply couldn't see how God could be both loving and powerful. In her mind, either God is powerful but not loving, since her children died; or He is a loving God who means well but isn't powerful.

"You're going to have to pick one!" she insisted. The pain in her eyes looked like a silent scream.

Many of us feel a pain so deep that we have no words for it. It comes when we cry out in primal agony . . . and heaven remains deathly silent.

I have sat side by side with a friend after she buried her child, and for hours neither of us spoke a word. It felt to me that any words would cheapen what she carried in her soul. She had waited for years for this little one, and in a moment, heaven received him.

To those of you who have tasted the depth of that kind of grief and loss, know that only Christ Himself understands the solitary, abandoned road you travel. But you are *not* alone! He has been there too. Please stay with me here—I don't say these things lightly. He has walked every step of this broken road, and He has gone where we could not go. Christ has tasted from an even deeper cup than yours. God turned out the lights on His own Son and let Him drink every drop of the cup of wrath by Himself on the darkest day this earth has ever known.

> "And on that day," declares the Lord God, "I will make the sun go down at noon and darken the earth in broad daylight." (Amos 8:9 ESV)

Immanuel's Orphaned Cry

At the crucifixion of Jesus Christ, Matthew tells us that "from the sixth hour there was darkness over all the land until the ninth hour. And about the ninth hour Jesus cried out with a loud voice, saying, 'Eli, Eli, lema sabachthani?' that is, 'My God, my God, why have you forsaken me?'" (27:45–46 ESV).

I can't begin to imagine what Christ faced during those three hours of darkness as He fought for breath. Leading up to His execution, He had been stripped and mocked, beaten bloody, His beard pulled out by the roots, His face a disfigured mess—but nothing, *nothing* He faced, could compare to those three dark hours. During those one hundred and eighty minutes, in an economy known only to the Godhead, Christ the sinless Lamb of God took on Himself the sin of the world:

> Every twisted thought of every perverted imagination.
> Every cutting, demeaning word ever spoken.
> Every heartless deception ever perpetrated.
> Every callous, heartless deed ever done.
> Every random act of gratuitous cruelty ever conceived by evil hearts.
> Every unspeakable atrocity ever committed.

He took it *all*. He took it for those who know they are broken and for those who pretend they are not. He took it for each one of us:

- The drunk driver who kills a child
- The desperate woman who takes the life of her unborn baby
- The criminal and the criminally insane
- The one who walks onto a school campus and opens fire
- The rape victim
- The abused
- The battered
- The abandoned

Christ took the full force of the brokenness of this world and for love of you and me became the abandoned One. Elizabeth Barrett Browning described what took place on the cross as Immanuel shouted His orphaned cry:

> *Deserted! God could separate from His own essence rather;*
> *And Adam's sins have swept between the righteous Son and Father:*
> *Yea, once, Immanuel's orphaned cry His universe hath shaken—*
> *It went up single, echoless, "My God, I am forsaken!"*[13]

On the cross—alone, abandoned, forsaken—Jesus Christ asked the *why?* for us all. Remember the chilling words? "Why have You forsaken Me?"

What went wrong? Why did this happen?

The answer may sound cold and heartless, but it is most certainly neither.

Someone had to pay.

Someone had to lay down the ransom price for our sin and rebellion, or we would stay mired in our own wicked misery forever. Only One could pay that price—only Christ, the spotless Lamb of God. Only He had led a sinless life. And only He could agree with His Father before time began to sacrifice His own pristine life to save our own wretched ones.

We will never know what it meant for Christ to have His own Father throw Him into that cauldron of deepest evil. We do know that it so unhinged the workings of the universe that even the sun refused to shine as God the Father turned away from His Son. As Jesus bore the sin of the world, He endured an indescribable abandonment. The innocent shed His blood for the guilty.

There simply was no other way.

Millennia before, when Adam and Eve disobeyed God and ate from the Tree of Knowledge of Good and Evil, their sin ripped a chasm between a holy God and a broken people. They felt it in the garden: abandoned, alone, ashamed. Since then, each one of us has felt it, and so we have cried out, "Why?"

As Christ plunged into the darkness of that evil, He paid for every sin ever committed, from that first one to the last one that ever will darken this world. Not only did He pay the price in full; He redeemed every broken piece.

Just as Adam and Eve took and ate—and so we all feel the abandonment of the orphan's cry—so Christ said on the night His friend betrayed Him, "This is my body, broken for you, take and eat" (see chapter 13). And so He made it possible for us all to come home through faith in Him and in His finished work on the cross.

On the cross, Jesus uttered the question that so many of us have asked of God in our own darkest nights: "Why have You forsaken me?" The question hung in the air, suspended, as if held there by pure, raw, uncomprehending agony. And yet that wasn't the last thing our Lord uttered. "It is finished!" He cried (John 19:30) a little later. And then, finally, "Father, into your hands I commit my spirit" (Luke 23:46).

From abandoned to embraced! And so shall it be for us—but not quite yet.

The Road Home

A few months ago I was in the Dominican Republic, driving to a World Vision area development project—a pregnancy clinic for moms and their new babies to teach young women how to care for their children. The village that houses the clinic sits on the border between the Dominican Republic and Haiti. The catastrophic earthquake that hit Haiti in 2010 did tremendous damage to many of the roads leading in and out of the country, and these poor countries simply lack the money or manpower to repair them all.

Still, we did pretty well . . . until we saw a detour sign leading off the main road and onto a dirt track. I have never been so thrown about in a vehicle in my entire life! Every pothole seemed bigger than the one before, and several times I banged my head on the roof of the truck. We eventually made it to the village, but we arrived pretty bruised and banged up.

That's how I see this road that you and I are on.

It can be a very, *very* rough road. But that sort of trip was never the original plan. God laid for us a smooth and beautiful road, but the detour out of the garden of Eden—across sun-seared deserts and over treacherous mountains, through raging rivers and finally up to a cross on a hill—is neither smooth nor beautiful. But it is the way home. Of that I remain utterly convinced.

To the greatest theological (yet desperately human) question of all, "Why doesn't God end suffering *now*?" I have no compelling answer. R. C. Sproul calls suffering "the Achilles' heel of the Christian faith." C. S. Lewis devoted a whole book to it, *The Problem of Pain* (which he wrote during an emotionally pleasant time. Read *A Grief Observed* to see how his approach changed when he had to travel over his own bumpy, rocky road). Many wonderful, scholarly works wrestle with this difficult issue.

But it's neither my ability nor my heart to tackle that issue here. My heart is to sit with you, right where you are, and share with you what I do believe. I am sure of far less now, as a woman of fifty-five, than I was as a young woman of twenty-five! But what I am sure of, I would stake my life on.

I believe with all my heart that God is both loving and sovereign.

I believe that the Lord created us with a free will so that we could choose to love Him or choose to walk away.

I believe that when Adam and Eve chose to disobey, we lost our perfect place in Eden.

I believe that God's fiery love for us is so overpowering that He willingly allowed His own Son to walk the hardest mile of all, in human shoes, to pay for our sin.

I believe that Christ chose to endure the most devastating agony and death any man or woman will ever face so that you and I can be forgiven.

I believe that when we weep, God catches every tear.

I believe that no pain is wasted, and that even out of the greatest trage-dies, God has promised He will bring good.

I believe that you have never lived an unloved moment in your life.

I believe He has been there too. You are not alone! You were not alone then, you are not alone now, and He will never, *ever* leave you.

Detours tend to kick up a lot of dust. Sometimes we can still see where we are going, while at other times the road seems to disappear—but always, Christ remains in control.

The Reality of a Cloudy Mirror

When the apostle Paul described our broken condition, he compared it to a faulty, fuzzy-looking glass: "Now we see things imperfectly as in a cloudy mirror, but then we will see everything with perfect clarity" (1 Corinthians 13:12 NLT).

The late Corrie Ten Boom, a Dutch evangelist and Holocaust survivor, once wrote about life as we see it from our perspective, full of tangled threads and knots, like a poorly crafted piece of embroidered cloth. Only God can see what the real picture looks like on the other side, an exquisite piece of rare and exceptional beauty, a crown of righteousness. I love that!

One of the most poignant lessons I've learned is that God is far more interested in who we are becoming than what we are doing. It's a great concept, but even thoughts like that can be hard to hold on to in the middle of a storm, when we can see only flashes of His face through the lightning.

When I study the lives of those who have asked the most powerful and searing *why* questions in all of Scripture, I see a scarlet thread of hope woven through each one.

Job, a righteous man decimated by one tragedy after another, hurled question after question at God. We hear this:

> I had only heard about you before, but now I have seen you with my own eyes. I take back everything I said, and I sit in dust and ashes to show my repentance. (42:5–6 NLT)

David, despite the knowledge that God had chosen him to rule as king over Israel, found himself hunted down and forced to live in a cave like a fugitive:

> Let all that I am praise the LORD; may I never forget the good things he does for me. He forgives all my sins and heals all my diseases. He redeems me from death and crowns me with love and tender mercies. (Psalm 103:2–4 NLT)

Paul, beaten and shipwrecked, stoned and left for dead, said:

> I am convinced that nothing can ever separate us from God's love. Neither death nor life, neither angels nor demons, neither our fears for today nor our worries about tomorrow—not even the powers of hell can separate us from God's love. No power in the sky above or in the earth below—indeed, nothing in all creation will ever be able to separate us from the love of God that is revealed in Christ Jesus our Lord. (Romans 8:38–39 NLT)

My human heart and mind can't understand God's ways, but I trust His heart. And I have had to fight a hard-won, bloodied war to get to this place of rest.

God never answered Job's questions, just as He may never answer yours on this side of eternity. But to every *why?* that has ever ripped your heart in two, remember that God gave us Easter morning!

On that first Easter morning so long ago, God introduced a new *why?* into our journey. It's the most glorious *why* of all:

Why do you look for the living among the dead? He is not here, he has risen! (Luke 24:5–6)

And my soul cries out: "He has risen indeed!"

FIVE

HIDING, PRETENDING, AND OTHER FAILED ESCAPES

Avoiding an Old Strategy That Never Works

In retrospect, I think the concert promoter thought it would be cute (and, I'm sure, cheap). It happened in my "rock-star" days back in the '80s.

If you're not familiar with my background, you might as well know that I haven't always been the mild-mannered woman you see on the back of this book. In fact, part of my résumé includes a stint as a Christian new-wave artist with jet-black, punky hair, dressed in leather. My son once saw an album cover with me in the aforementioned regalia, and after staring at it for some time, he asked only one question: "Mom, did you *mean* to look like that?"

"Yes, I did," I replied. "I was a new-wave artist."

"Wow . . . who were you waving at in a get-up like that?" he asked

On this particular night I was touring the United States with my British band. We had just finished a sold-out concert in Orlando, Florida, and the guys in my band were hungry. (But then, they were *always* hungry, and had already eaten twice that night, before the concert.) The promoter said he had a great idea for where to take us, just the place for the boys to eat as much as they wanted without him having to re-mortgage his home.

He took us to a pizza place called Chuck E. Cheese, "where a kid can be a kid." Perfect for the band!

Since we arrived near closing time, the place seemed fairly quiet. The guys got in line to order their pizza, while I grabbed a slice of cheese pizza and a Diet Coke. As I carried it to my table, someone tapped me on the shoulder. When I turned to see the person, I found myself facing a six-foot-tall mouse instead.

I screamed and threw my tray at him.

The whole restaurant went deathly silent. Apparently I had just soaked

Chuck E. with a soft drink and covered him in cheese—in his own establishment! The mask and costume intended to amuse and thrill had instead alarmed and terrified.

Send in the Clowns

Do you remember the *Seinfeld* episode where Kramer gets confronted by a clown?

"Are you still afraid of clowns?" the clown asks.

"Yes," Kramer whimpers.

Very funny stuff, but for me it went much deeper. I have always had a profound fear of people in masks. I don't mind costumes so long as I can see your face, but a covered face makes me panic. Only in recent years have I begun to understand why.

I trace it back to my father's brain aneurism that I described a bit in chapter 3. The last time I ever looked in his eyes before the authorities took him away, I saw a complete stranger. I couldn't see my father. To me, as a five-year-old child, he might as well have worn a terrifying Halloween mask. My dad had left me, leaving a monster in his place.

But do you know the ironic thing? Although masks terrify me, for years I wore one myself.

The Masks We Wear

As a teenager and into my twenties I never liked what I saw in the mirror. I tried to hide my bad skin with whatever cream I could get. I seem to remember a brand called Clearasil that came in two options, clear or skin tone . . . for anyone who was unfortunate enough to have orange skin! I ran up a huge credit card bill in college because I felt so bad about myself inside that I bought lots of new clothes to dress up the outside. It never worked, but I kept trying.

I didn't like my weight, but rather than just cut back on my eating, I searched for the "magic" diet or pill that would "fix" me. We didn't have a bathroom scale, so I went to our local butcher and asked him to weigh me. I reckoned that if he could weigh a whole cow, he could handle me. I have tried every diet on the planet, at least five times. They all work.

I didn't. When the problem lies deep in the cellar of your soul, no window dressing will help.

I think we all wear masks in one way or another. It's our way of trying to fit in, to belong. The more broken we feel inside, the more we feel compelled to hide our brokenness from others so they don't laugh at us or reject us. Over the last sixteen years I've spoken to more than four million women from the platform at Women of Faith. I hear the same things over and over:

"I don't like the way I look."

"I don't like the way I feel."

"I hate what I see in the mirror."

"If people knew the real me, no one would want to know me."

"How can God love me after all the things I have done?"

"How can God forgive me if I can't forgive myself?"

It breaks my heart to know that although Christ died to bring us freedom, so often we followers of Christ seem the least free of all. It begins by feeling judged by the standards of our culture (and found wanting). Add to that the judgment of the Christian community—of the church—heaped on top, and it's enough to sink the *QE2*. "Merciless" doesn't begin to describe it.

Do you remember in the book of John where the Pharisees and teachers of the law dragged a woman caught in the act of adultery before Jesus? They threw her down into the dust like a bundle of rags and drew a circle of condemnation all around her. I remember watching the same thing happen to a friend of mine. Her marriage had ended, and as she struggled to find help and hope, she found herself thrown inside a circle of accusers. They didn't want to listen; they only wanted to tell her what to do.

What makes us so comfortable with a circle?

Is it that we have left no way out?

Is it that we get to look over the head of the broken into the eyes of those we think are just like us?

Whatever it is, Christ Himself stepped into the circle that day—and broke it into pieces. How did He do it? He simply invited those who had never sinned to throw the first stone. Very offensive stuff to the crowd, for it implied that the sin of the one who threw her on the ground was just as bad as the sin of the woman in the dust! I'm sure none of them liked the taste of that, as one by one they dropped their carefully selected stones and skulked away.

I find it sad that no one came to sit beside her.

No one "got" the radical truth that Christ proclaimed, that all of us are deeply messed up and broken, each in our different ways. And they missed something else too: they missed the truth that God has all the experience in the world in dealing with broken people and loves them dearly and deeply.

Have you ever fallen victim to the sort of judgment described in John 8? If so, no doubt it tended to keep you hiding in the cellar because your accusers made it so *very* clear that that's where you belonged. (And if you dared to come out, they were waiting with sharp stones.)

If you find yourself in this situation, let me make a suggestion. Open the cellar door at least far enough to admit this truth: as you are *right now*, with all your struggles, secrets, and the masks that hide you from view, God passionately loves you. He knows your "stuff." He sees your pain. He invites you to come to Him, just as you are—exactly as you are at this very broken moment.

Yes, it will take some courage. Some people around you may not like it. It might even feel "wrong" because, let's face it: you're been hiding in that musty cellar for a long, long time.

The Stampede into Hiding

We come by hiding naturally—or maybe, quite normally, although very *un*naturally:

> And they heard the sound of the Lord God walking in the garden in the cool of the day, and the man and his wife hid themselves from the presence of the Lord God among the trees of the garden. (Genesis 3:8 ESV)

In that moment, Adam and Eve found themselves doing something that no human being had ever done before. *They were hiding.* They had never heard the word *hide*. They had no such word in their vocabulary. To hide meant deception—pretending not to be where you really were. But they didn't know the words *deception* or *pretending* either. All they had known— their whole experience of existence—was the joy of being alive, loved, and greatly treasured. Treasured by their Creator and Friend, and treasured by one another.

Can you picture what it must have felt like to stroll with God in the late afternoon, day after day (perhaps year after year, we have no way of knowing). I've tried to imagine this and can't quite wrap my mind around it. To savor the cooling breeze, bearing the delicious fragrance of fruit-laden orchards and wild flowers beyond imagination . . . to enjoy the matchless beauty bathed in the golden light of late afternoon, fading softly into twilight . . . to casually and sweetly chat with the Creator of the universe, sharing the little events (and humorous moments) of the day.

But then, like a sucker punch to the gut, their perfect spring ended, winter fell iron hard, and it was over. Paradise closed its doors to Adam and Eve. From the moment our first parents tasted the forbidden fruit, everything changed. The serpent had told them that eating it would "open their eyes," and what a cruel, cynical twisting of the truth that turned out to be. "For God knows that when you eat of it your eyes will be opened, and you will be like God, knowing good and evil" (Genesis 3:5).

Well, it wasn't *all* a lie (many of his falsehoods carry a grain of distorted truth). The first part of the tempter's statement was true. Their eyes *were* opened—but what did they see?

They saw their nakedness.

They saw their guilt.

They saw their pitiful, broken selves.

As Derek Kidner wrote in his commentary on Genesis, "What a grotesque anticlimax to the dream of enlightenment."[14] They now knew of their nakedness and felt deeply ashamed. And there was another new emotion! Shame had never afflicted them in all their days . . . until now.

This all reminds me of what I consider the most insidious aspects of sin: Even if we admit our error, even if we turn from our sin, we can't unlearn what we have learned. We can't undo what we have done. We can't unknow what we know.

For Adam and Eve, every moment brought a fresh reminder of the disaster they had brought upon themselves. Where once they had walked in sunshine, now they lived in shadows—dark corners of doubt and worry and fear. And questions, so many questions. How sick they must have felt inside!

And then they heard God walking in the garden. Just a short time before, that would have been the most welcoming, beautiful sound of their lives. And now it made their hearts stutter.

They were afraid.

They didn't know the name of this fear, but they felt its cruel, iron grip.

You know that feeling too. It may come with a call from a doctor's office, in a letter in the mail, in a conversation with a friend who says, "I have something I need to tell you." The fear and dread wash over you, and you feel so powerless, so helpless. But this fear struck Adam and Eve as a totally new and sickening experience. How would they respond?

Their first instinct sounds all too familiar.

They didn't run to God, throw themselves at His feet, and pour out their hearts to Him, explaining everything that had happened. Instead, they ran away. They hid.

Such is the sad, ugly legacy of brokenness.

Sin makes us want to hide from the only One who can help us—the only One who can save us. Of course, the serpent intended this very thing all along, to break the special bond that existed between God and His beloved creation.

I tell my son, Christian, many things; but one of the most important things I tell him, I repeat over and over: "The bigger the mess, the faster you run to us." Tragically, the trust broken in Eden makes it *so* hard for us to do that.

Think about it. When you feel you've made a mess of things, that you've fallen and failed God in some way, how do you normally respond? Most of us want to hide. We want to run away and try to get our act together or fix ourselves up a bit. *Then*, we tell ourselves, we'll go to God and explain everything.

It didn't work in the garden and it works no better now.

Adam and Eve tried to cover their nakedness by making clothing out of fig leaves, the largest covering they could find. They may have covered their nakedness from each other, but they couldn't cover their sin and shame. They couldn't hide their broken condition from God. They had taken part in a diabolical exchange that turned beauty into ashes. Although God had made trees to delight their eyes and excite their palate (see Genesis 2:9), now those very trees became their cellar . . . their dark place to hide.

What about you? We all have favorite places to hide.

Some hide in food. Have you ever done this? Perhaps you've built a wall of flesh around your broken heart to keep people at a distance. When you looked a certain way, you may believe that you were used or abused because of your appearance, and since then you have done everything in your power to hide yourself somewhere, tucked deep inside. Food may be the only thing over which you feel you have some control. It has become your secret weapon—so you choose to use it, disappearing a little more every day.

Some hide in "stuff." Ever tried that? You think, *Just one more pair of shoes, one more handbag, one more dress, and I'll feel better.* It can be makeup, a new dress, or an elegant necklace—we never feel satisfied; we just need to try "one more thing." But "things" will never make us happy, no matter how good the ad campaign.

As I mentioned earlier, one of my dearest friends is Dr. Henry Cloud. He is a clinical psychologist and a passionate student of the Word of God. He told me recently of a study that the head of the American Psychiatric Association commissioned several years ago to investigate what makes people happy. The final results seem shocking . . . unless you study the Word of God. It became crystal clear that only 10 percent of things that make people genuinely happy come from the outside. Even then, those things give only a temporary bump, and then people return to their set point. So the new car, the house, the dress, or the ring—whatever it might be that we think, *If I just had that, I would be so much happier*—can't do what we hoped it would do.

Some hide in relationships. Are you there now? Maybe you go through relationships quickly, finding fault with the other person, sure that whatever "issue" arises, it must be him. He just doesn't make you feel the way you want to feel, so you move on. But the trouble is, you take you wherever you go.

Some hide in religion. This one looks good . . . from the outside. It's all about appearance, all about being in the right place at the right time, all about the approval of others. It's all about being *seen* as good, but knowing absolutely nothing of the freedom or joy that an actual and vital relationship with Christ can bring.

Some hide in ministry. This was my hiding place of choice. I seemed to "be there" for everyone else, but no one got to see the real me. I felt that if I helped you, prayed with you, shared God's love with you, I had to be okay. I just never let you take a close look at me, in case you might see that, in fact, I was far from okay.

We hide, of course, in a wild variety of ways. I've listed only a few. You may have chosen a different place, a different method, a different cellar to climb into. Perhaps your hiding places seem so murky and dark you can't even identify them. Even so, God asks each of us who is hiding the very same question He asked Adam and Eve.

The Question

Shortly after Adam sinned, God called out to him and asked, "Where are you?" (Genesis 3:9). The Bible doesn't give us the Lord's inflection when He called to Adam. But I don't think it sounded accusatory, like, "Where *are* you, anyway?"

I think the voice sounded sad.

I also think the question was full of grace. The Lord didn't ask, "Why are you hiding?" He asked instead, "Where are you?"

Can you hear the difference? If God had asked *why?* it would have pushed Adam and Eve deeper into the forest and further into their shame. So He asked *where?* Such a question tends to call us out of hiding. That was the heart of God to Adam and Eve, and it is His heart to each of us today.

I find it very telling that Adam responded to the question God did *not* ask. He replied as though God had asked him why he hid: "I heard the sound of you in the garden, and I was afraid, because I was naked, and I hid myself."

Isn't that amazing! The shame brought on by sin and brokenness can have a more convincing voice than that of God Himself.

I know this is true in my own life. So often God asks me *where?* and I answer *why?* So don't feel surprised that you beat yourself up when you know you have fallen short of what God wants from you and for your life! That's exactly what happened to the only two human beings (other than Christ) who have ever walked in perfect relationship with our Father. Part of the challenge of our brokenness is to train our hearts to hear God's love above the din of our shame.

Adam and Eve could not disguise their futile attempt at hiding; their brokenness was written all over them. (Who were these people—crouching in the bushes, hearts pounding, faces twisted with fear?) Yet brokenness has many disguises, and over the years we have become quite adept at trying to make it appear like something else.

The Urge to Pretend

A friend asked me to fill in at the last moment as a speaker for a very fancy luncheon in Palm Springs, California. As far as I was concerned, I had neither the desire nor the ability to do it; at that point I had never spoken in public, despite my background in television and music.

But then she said, "Oh, Sheila, I'm really stuck."

"Marlene," I countered, "you personally know half the female speakers in America. Ask one of them."

To which she replied—and I quote word for word—"I've asked everyone else. You're the bottom of the barrel."

Wow. Isn't *that* a confidence builder?

As I drove to the event, I had quite a heart-to-heart with the Lord.

"I would just like to apologize up front, Lord. You are not going to look good today!"

So I showed up. The experience overwhelmed me more than I ever imagined it would. I sat at the head table and surveyed the surreal scene around me. About a thousand women had come, all of them immaculately dressed . . . interestingly enough, with faces that didn't move (plastic surgery humor). I couldn't help staring at the woman to my left—tall, slender, blonde, and just stunning. The kind of woman who makes you say, *"Really, Lord? Share the love a little!"*

So I spoke. I didn't quite know what to talk about, so I decided to put them all off their dessert and talk about what happened when my tidy little world collapsed and I ended up in a psych ward. The room became *very* still. I had no idea what they were thinking or feeling, but when I finished speaking, the first woman to approach me was the beautiful blonde sitting next to me. She took off the two diamond-encrusted gold cuffs she wore and showed me where she had slit her wrists in a botched suicide attempt.

I had no idea that one could package pain so beautifully. But as tears flowed down her cheeks, I realized that you can't Botox pain. You can't Botox brokenness.

That day opened my eyes like never before. I had *no* idea. On the surface, this woman's life looked perfect. I'm sure that many in the room envied her—but the pain inside so overwhelmed her that she tried ending her life to stop the charade. I imagine that her wealth made it possible to chase so many of the dreams that we are told will make us happy. How dis-illusioning to find every one of them fatally flawed!

I saw her suicide attempt as a way of screaming out, "This is all a lie!" It reminded me of the Hans Christian Andersen tale about the emperor who didn't dress quite as well as he thought. Do you remember the story?

A very vain emperor fell for the lies of two smooth swindlers. They said they could weave the finest cloth in the land, but only the wise could see it; it would remain invisible to fools. For days, they pretended to work on the looms with no thread at all. Everyone in the kingdom knew of the supposed magic power of the cloth and couldn't wait to see which of their neighbors would turn out to be the greatest fool.

The emperor grew impatient to see the cloth, but felt afraid to ask to see it, in case the cloth proved invisible to him. So he sent an old minister.

The minister felt horrified when he realized he couldn't see it, but rather than admit his inability, he declared it to be the finest cloth he had ever seen. Finally the weavers declared the outfit ready, and although the emperor couldn't see a thing, he pretended to be thrilled with how he looked. As he led a grand processional down the main street in town, a small, innocent child finally cried out, "But he hasn't got anything on!"

Pretending that something works doesn't make it work. In fact, it can drive you crazy. And it can make denial the only place left to live.

What Would I Talk About?

My mother-in-law, Eleanor, was quite a character. She had fiery red hair, a temperament to match, and an enviable comfort level about sharing her thoughts freely with others. My mum swings to the other side of the pendulum and at times won't speak up when to speak up might be both healthy and helpful.

I remember the first time Eleanor stood about an inch from my nose and shared her opinion, very loudly, in my face. It surprised me, almost shocked me. At other times she would refuse to speak to me at all, which bothered Barry even more.

One evening when William, Barry, Eleanor, and I were returning from quite an animated dinner, Barry suggested to his mom that talking to a counselor can often provide real help. He told her that he and I have spoken with counselors both individually and together, especially when we found ourselves stuck on some issue. I will never forget the look on her face as she turned round, looked both of us in the face, and said, "What on earth would I have to talk to a counselor about?"

William almost drove off the road, he laughed so hard.

A Perfect Fit

The truth is that we all are broken at some level. Some of us know it and have no idea what to do about it, while some are deeply unaware, although at times we feel a distant rumble in our souls. To each one of us, God's answer is Christ.

When our loving Father saw the pathetic attempt Adam and Eve made to cover themselves, He said, "That will never do." Scripture says, "And the LORD God made clothing from animal skins for Adam and his wife" (Genesis 3:21). They would indeed be covered, but something had to die to accomplish that. Such a beautiful foreshadowing of Christ, who would shed His blood to cover us all!

You don't have to hide anymore. You are loved as you are. You needn't wear a mask; God sees you as you are. You don't have to pretend to be okay; Christ is our righteousness, and we get to be human after all, to be real, to be loved, to be free. You don't have to deny the truth; the Lord knows it all and offers you Christ.

If you will dare to try on this outfit that God has made for you, in no time at all you will begin to see the truth: it's a perfect fit.

SIX

What Can I Know for Sure?

Three Rock-Solid Truths to Keep You Standing, Whatever Happens

As I write these words, autumn has arrived. We had such a dry and hot summer this year that when I look around I don't see the kind of color change I normally expect. But the temperature has dropped, and the days have grown shorter. Those are winter's calling cards, sent out in advance. The real thing is just around the corner.

Life, too, has its seasons, just as the calendar does.

But no, that's not quite accurate, is it? It isn't "just like" the calendar. The calendar is predictable and sequential. Tuesday follows Monday, December follows November, and winter follows autumn. But it doesn't work that way in life. In life, seasons can change in a single hour or a single moment. Seasons can change with the ring of a telephone.

You can be enjoying a glorious, sun-splashed season of happiness and contentment one moment, when suddenly a new season intrudes, without warning, suddenly changing *everything*.

Right now we're going through a season as a family of so many of our dear friends facing drastic medical situations. Two children in Christian's school have been diagnosed with cancer, and in our close circle of friends, three young adults have malignant brain tumors.

To be honest, I've never known a time like this before. Bad news seems to buzz around us like a swarm of bees.

When difficult seasons like this hit, we often don't know what to do. Much of the time, we don't even know what to *think*. We long for a little solidity and security, some firm place to plant our feet while the earth below us trembles and shifts.

When I talk to women who find themselves in this sort of season of upheaval, they usually wind up asking, in one form or another, "What can I know for sure?" If all else falls away, what can they grab hold of and know beyond all doubt will remain secure and solid and true?

In these seasons of change, perplexity, and stress, I believe there truly are things we can know for sure. I can think of at least three.

Nothing Surprises God

As human beings, we have no early warning system for trouble or tragedy. Most of the time, we get no heads-up before trouble drops out of a clear blue sky. With God, however, there are no surprises. Zero. None. He knows what lies around every corner and just behind every horizon. We don't see trouble coming, but He does and knows just what to do about it.

The Trammels didn't see their change of seasons coming, but then again, we almost never do, do we? One morning he was Brent Trammel as he's always been: funny, laid-back, hardworking. But by the next morning—Monday, December 6, 2010—everything had changed.

His boys noticed it first as he got ready to take them to school. His speech sounded a little slurred, and he confused some names. Immediately concerned, his wife, Jennalee, took him to the emergency room.

After many tests, doctors determined that Brent had suffered a seizure, caused by a tumor on his brain's left temporal lobe.

I should back up a little and tell you a bit about this amazing family. Brent and Jennalee Trammel have three boys, Chase, Cole, and Tate. Until recently, we lived just four houses apart. Christian and Chase are about the same age, so I always knew that if Christian wasn't at our house, he was at Chase's, and vice versa. Jennalee and I spent many summer nights sitting in our sports chairs in one of our driveways, watching the boys ride their bikes or skateboards and patching up a multitude of war wounds. It's a family joke that the Trammels have had more than their fair share of disasters—including broken bones and a burst water pipe gushing from an upstairs bathroom to soak the hardwood floors beneath.

But this?

How could a season change this quickly? It left us all breathless.

If you have ever lived through this kind of season, you'll understand what

I'm about to say. God does mysterious things in the midst of unexpected seasons, possibly altering the very landscape of your life. I have and continue to see this in Brent.

When doctors confirmed the tumor diagnosis, Brent said to Jennalee, "Maybe I was created for this very moment." On his CaringBridge website (a site created for those who face serious illness, where they can post updates and family and friends can leave notes of encouragement), he quoted this text: "But I have raised you up for this very purpose, that I might show you my power and that my name might be proclaimed in all the earth" (Exodus 9:16). In that post, Brent declared his firm belief in God's sovereignty at work, even in this unexpected and unwelcome season of his life. And that leads to the first thing we can know for sure when life seems to come unraveled:

1. Nothing that happens surprises God, so trust Him in the midst of your pain.

The Bible presents God as sovereign over all of history . . . including *your* history. While that doesn't necessarily mean that He "caused" your difficult circumstances—God rarely privileges us with that sort of information—it does mean He will strengthen you to glorify Him through whatever comes your way. He saw it coming, He knows what's coming next, and He asks you to trust Him in the midst of it all.

The prophet Isaiah longed for his countrymen to "get" this lesson. He even started out one of his talks on the topic by telling them, "Remember this, fix it in mind, take it to heart" (Isaiah 46:8). When a mouthpiece of the Lord almighty says something like *that* to you, you had better sit up, stop playing with your iPhone, and pay careful attention! And then he continued, speaking for God:

> Remember the former things, those of long ago;
> I am God, and there is no other;
> I am God, and there is none like me.
> I make known the end from the beginning,
> from ancient times, what is still to come.
> I say: My purpose will stand,
> and I will do all that I please.

(vv. 9–10)

Nothing catches God off guard. Nothing blindsides Him. Nothing derails His ultimate purposes. God knows "what is still to come," and He declares about it, "My purpose will stand, and I will do all that I please."

When we first encounter that passage, our minds may go to hurricanes, tsunamis, or earthshaking geopolitical events. It's true, God does know those things, and He knew them before He ever formed the world.

But don't miss this: God's words also apply to *you*.

He knows your life, your history, and your future, too—right down to the tiniest detail. God knows what is still to come in *your* life, and He declares to you that His purpose for you will stand. *In your life* He will do everything that pleases Him.

Jesus gives me a picture of what this looks like in "real life." Just hours before His betrayal and arrest, He told His disciples (minus Judas) that one of the Twelve would "lift up his heel" against Him, in fulfillment of a prophecy in Psalm 41:9. And then He said, "I am telling you now before it happens, so that when it does happen you will believe that I am He" (John 13:19).

The betrayal of Judas must have shocked the other eleven disciples right to their core. *Judas? Betraying the Lord? No! How could it be?* But it didn't catch Jesus by surprise; John wrote that Jesus knew from the beginning who did not believe and who would betray Him (John 6:64). Even though none of His men understood His meaning until after all the events of Calvary had unfolded, still Jesus told them what would happen so that, in the aftermath of their shock and grief, they would believe that He really was the Messiah. None of them expected an arrested, mocked, beaten, crucified, and buried Messiah. It was unthinkable! Such a dark scenario simply never occurred to them. But Jesus wanted them to know He had seen it all coming, so that once they regained their equilibrium, they might once again start to put the pieces together and eventually fulfill the task He had given them in happier times.

After predicting the treachery of Judas, Jesus bewildered His little band of followers even further when He announced that the hour of His departure had come.

He would have to leave them, He declared; and although they didn't understand most of what He told them, the mere sound of it disturbed them deeply. Once again, He followed up with His reason for telling them: "I have told you now before it happens, so that when it does happen you will believe" (John 14:29). Jesus had full knowledge of the mayhem and pain to come, and He wanted to reassure His dearly loved followers that none of it took Him by surprise, none of it meant God had abandoned them, and none of it indicated they had believed in vain. Twice Jesus told His disciples what was about to happen, so the searing fire even then rushing toward them wouldn't incinerate their faith.

I believe Brent Trammel well understands this lesson, and that is why he can commit his unknown future to a known God.

Our conversations with the Trammels have changed in the last few months. We still talk about the boys and how they're doing at school and homework challenges, but inevitably our talk turns toward Brent's battle and how it impacts Jennalee and the three boys. When this kind of challenge hits a family, the ripples extend far beyond the person who feels tossed into the water, like a stone snatched from the shore and thrown into the pond. I have watched as the Trammels have cast themselves on God for comfort and strength. Perhaps when we imagine ourselves to be strong, we forget how weak we really are.

When Brent knew he would face brain surgery before Christmas, he posted on his CaringBridge site a passage that reaffirmed his confidence in God's sovereign rule, and that he had determined to rest in it:

> Do not be anxious about anything, but in everything by prayer and supplication with thanksgiving let your requests be made known to God. And the peace of God, which surpasses all understanding, will guard your hearts and your minds in Christ Jesus. (Philippians 4:6–7 ESV)

On December 15, a crowd of us gathered with Brent and Jennalee in our pastor's study to pray for Brent, his doctors, and the surgery scheduled for the following Friday morning. I love Jack Graham, our pastor, a wonderful teacher with a tender pastor's heart. I will never forget that night as many of us knelt around Brent and Jennalee and with tears asked God to do what only God can do. And we read what Brent had chosen as his verses for that day:

> That is why we never give up. Though our bodies are dying, our spirits are being renewed every day. For our present troubles are small and won't last very long. Yet they produce for us a glory that vastly outweighs them and will last forever! (2 Corinthians 4:16–17 NLT)

And so together we prepared for Brent's surgery. Only one question remained.

What's next?

Nothing Can Separate You from God's Love

Scans showed clearly that Brent had a mass on his brain, but the doctor wouldn't know until the surgery what kind of tumor they were dealing with. We prayed for it to be benign. At 4:00 a.m. on the morning of his surgery, Brent wrote a note to his boys just before he left the house and posted it on his CaringBridge site. Here is an excerpt:

> Chase, Cole, and Tate,
>
> It is very early (4 AM) and God is at work! I wanted to just take a few moments to let you know how much I love each one of you! You have each made me the happiest dad in the entire world . . . we were never called to walk a faithless, simple life but a life full of abundance and grace that only God can give. This morning, Dad will leave for the hospital without any fear of the unknown, and expect miracles to happen. NO MATTER the outcome of the procedure or the diagnosis, GOD IS IN CONTROL and HE will be praised!
>
> Below is one of my favorite verses: "For I am sure that neither death nor life, nor angels nor rulers, nor things present nor things to come, nor powers, nor height nor depth, nor anything else in all creation, will be able to separate us from the love of God in Christ Jesus our Lord" (Romans 8:38–39).
>
> No Fear, Jesus Never Fails,
>
> Dad

The truth of the sovereignty of God has the power to calm our fears and give us hope only when it joins hands with the truth of God's eternal love for us. How overwhelmingly grateful we should feel that the Bible consistently teaches *both* doctrines, from Genesis all the way to Revelation! And that leads us to the second thing we can know for sure regardless of what happens in our lives:

2. *God loves you, and nothing can separate you from His love.*

Suffering, pain, hardship, and tragedy all have a tendency to lie to us. In the darkness they whisper to our tortured souls, "Where is your God now?" or "Faith is nothing but wishful thinking, and this proves it," or "If there is a God, how could you still think He loves you? Would a loving God allow *this*?" When those doubts and lies creep into your head, how do you answer them?

I sometimes regret that most of us quote Romans 8:38–39 without considering the whole context of the passage. It doesn't really flow like we might have expected it to. Paul begins by asking, "If God is for us, who can be against us?" (v. 31). That being said, it *seems* like he's suggesting that no one and nothing can oppose us. And then he follows up by asking, "Who shall separate us from the love of Christ? Shall trouble or hardship or persecution or famine or nakedness or danger or sword?" (v. 35). Again, it *seems* like the answer must be, "Nothing and no one!"

But there is a whiplash coming. Suddenly the passage seems to veer off course. The way I read it, it *feels* like we should immediately go on to read about victory, conquest, success, joy, and rapture. And how I would like *that*! But that is *not* what Paul wrote next. Instead the scripture says,

> As it is written, "For your sake we face death all day long; we are considered as sheep to be slaughtered." (v. 36)

Face death? Sheep to be slaughtered? Is that supposed to encourage me? Does that sound like victory, conquest, success, joy, and rapture to *you*? Does that sound like a lack of opposition? I've sometimes wondered, *If that's a picture of success, then what constitutes failure? If that doesn't picture people who are against us, I hope it doesn't picture people who are for us.*

It does *seem* to interrupt the flow of Paul's message, doesn't it?

It does *feel* like a detour.

But it's really neither an interruption nor a detour. For Paul then wrote, "No, *in all these things*"—that is, death, slaughter, famine, nakedness, sword, and all the rest—"we are more than conquerors through him who loved us" (v. 37, emphasis added). He meant that even when people do oppose us, even when they do manage to starve us, strip us, savage us, and slay us, yet we remain "more than conquerors" *through Him who loved us.*

It doesn't "feel" like that, but it is true nonetheless. In times of great sorrow or trial, it isn't productive to deny or ignore your feelings. But don't hand them the steering wheel either! Instead, remember what Paul says here.

None of us are "conquerors" on our own, let alone "more than" conquerors. What does it mean to be "more than" a conqueror? Well, conquerors win battles and sometimes wars. They take over someone else's territory . . . for a time. And that's the best they can do.

To be "more than a conqueror" means that you do more than win temporal battles, wars, or territory. What you win, you win forever; and if you are connected to Christ, you win *everything*, quite literally. Not just isolated battles or solitary wars or bits of territory (for a little while), but the whole shebang, for eternity.

And over the whole thing is Christ's love. The fierce, unchanging, passionate love of Jesus.

Paul looks forward in this beautiful passage, and so must we. It makes sense in no other way. And so we wait for its full and final fulfillment.

With Us Through the Fire

As we waited in the intensive care unit that day after Brent's surgery, we wondered what new diagnosis would come from the operating room. Wendy, Jennalee's best friend since school, never left her side. Eventually we received news that Brent had come through the surgery well.

That was good, but no diagnosis quite yet.

Our wait would have to continue.

Three days before Christmas, we received the news for which we had waited. Brent's doctor confirmed that he had an oligodendroglioma tumor, grade 2, a fairly aggressive cancer. What a difficult diagnosis to hear! Everything the family had taken for granted a few weeks before changed in just moments.

Although Brent's family found the news very hard to receive, he displayed a peculiar grace and peace in the midst of it all. When this kind of fire takes your normal schedule and to-do list and reduces them to ashes, "normal" gets wiped off the table. Many things that used to seem so important become trivial and even foolish. Things you used to worry about no longer make so much as a blip on the radar of your mind.

What remains is a quiet focus on what really matters.

I admire Brent and Jennalee as they walk through these uncertain days. Among other things, I admire them for their commitment to tell the truth—they radiate complete confidence in Christ, without the slightest sugarcoating about what's happening. Jennalee, a gifted interior decorator, has created a beautiful home; and yet shortly after Christmas they decided to put it on the market to relieve some financial strain.

"Home is wherever the five of us are," Jennalee wrote on the family's web page. "The house doesn't matter."

As I watch the ongoing battle Brent faces, I see the purity of his faith shine a little brighter. It's as if his hearing has been fine-tuned to a Father who never takes His eyes off him and never stops telling him that He loves him—oh, how He loves him, no matter what any test result may say! Brent knows, down to the very core of his being, that God will stay with him throughout whatever comes next. And that brings me to the third and final thing we can know for sure when we face serious troubles of various kinds:

3. God will be with you always, and whatever you have to face, He will go through it with you.

Two precious passages of Scripture come immediately to mind. I have learned to count on the promise of Hebrews 13:5–6, and I hold on to it with everything in me. It tells me,

> God has said, "Never will I leave you; never will I forsake you." So we say with confidence, "The Lord is my helper; I will not be afraid. What can man do to me?"

We've seen this kind of logic before, in the passage about God's love from Romans 8. The writer asks, "What can man do to me?" *Seriously?* What kind of question is that? Man can do all sorts of things to me. He can bully me, insult me, threaten me. He can divorce me, abuse me, abandon me, injure me, cripple me. He can bankrupt me, jail me, kill me. But what he can't do, what he can never do, is make God leave me.

No one in the universe can do that.

When God promises, "Never will I leave you; never will I forsake you," you never have to worry about being left alone, ever again. You will never, in time or eternity, be all alone. And when God says He will help you, He means that His constant presence goes far beyond merely speculating; He means that His ever-present hand is there to grab you, hold you, and give you whatever assistance you require, right up to and beyond the moment He uses that hand to bring you to heaven to live with Him forever.

Brent Trammel banks on that promise. So does his wife. So do his boys. And they also depend on God's guarantee spoken through the prophet Isaiah:

> Fear not, for I have redeemed you;
>> I have summoned you by name; you are mine.
> When you pass through the waters,
>> I will be with you;
> and when you pass through the rivers,
>> they will not sweep over you.
> When you walk through the fire,
>> you will not be burned;
>> the flames will not set you ablaze.
> For I am the LORD, your God,
>> the Holy One of Israel, your Savior.

(ISAIAH 43:1–3)

Some skeptics might consider such words to be just a mental trick—an emotional crutch—to give comfort to clueless people of faith who have no other comfort in reach.

And so they mock.

Let them mock.

Brent and Jennalee and Cole and Chase and Tate and Sheila Walsh and millions of other followers of Christ through the centuries know these words to be rock-solid, divine guarantees that the Lord will remain with us through everything, always.

Everything.

Always.

Although no one would ever sign up for such a devastating experience as the one the Trammels now endure, many of those who have walked through the fire and the flood tell how God's presence has become sweeter to them than ever before.

Maybe that's what we mean by "bittersweet."

A Prayer for You

As I write, I pause for a moment to pray for you, dear reader. I don't know what you face right now. It may be all you can do to keep turning pages in this book. Perhaps you have arrived in a season where you feel blown all over the place. So many demands on your time and energy, and just when you seem to catch your breath, another sharp blast knocks you off your feet.

Or it may be far worse than that. You may be living in the aftermath of an absolute disaster. In a moment, everything you counted on and stood on got blown into a million pieces. Your life will never be the same again.

The death of a spouse

The death of a marriage

The loss of a job

So many things can pull the ground out from beneath your feet, without you seeing them coming. Perhaps you would use the word *consumed* to describe your life right now. The crisis might be financial, your health, relationships—but just as surely as fire mercilessly destroys everything in its wake, that is where you sit right now, devastated, alone, shocked.

I would never think of trying to minimize your pain (too many people over the years have done that to me). But if you're asking the question that so many have asked me—"What can I know for sure?"—then you already know my response.

Nothing that happens surprises God, so trust Him in the midst of your pain.

God loves you, and nothing can separate you from His love.

God will be with you always, and whatever you have to face, He will go through it with you.

Do you believe those things? If you do, then STAND there. Stand on the Rock. Stand, when your knees buckle and your tears fall like rain. Stand when everything else gives way. You can do that, I know, because Jesus Himself continues to stand with you. Forever.

A Tale of Two Teresas
Time-Tested Wisdom for Dealing with Persistent Pain

Elizabeth—or Betty, as her friends know her—lives in a small stone cottage in Scotland. She just turned eighty-two and has raised three children by herself since her husband died at age thirty-four. She may be eighty-two, but this year she has three things on her Christmas list: a bike, a dog, and a piano. Each one is so her and so unlikely that it makes me smile.

She is my mother.

I'm not sure exactly when my mum stopped being simply my mum to me and I began to see her separately as a woman who has walked through her own tragedy and heartbreak. As a little girl I felt acutely aware that I had no dad, but it didn't always occur to me that this meant my mum had no husband. Many times, however, we became painfully aware that our little family differed markedly from others.

Every Christmas Eve, for example, a deacon from our church arrived with a big box. Inside we'd find a turkey with all the trimmings and lots of treats for my brother, my sister, and me, goodies that the church knew my mum could not afford to buy. Sometimes one of Mum's friends would pop over with some secondhand clothes or shoes. One couple in our church paid for my teenage brother's driving lessons. Despite her thankfulness for the kindness of our friends and family, my mum still faced a great deal of hardship and loneliness as a widow who never remarried.

Just before I sat down to write this chapter, I called home and chatted with Mum. I pictured her sitting in her favorite armchair by the fire. During our conversation, she asked me, "Do you realize it's been fifty years since your dad died?"

Fifty years.

That's a long time to turn over in the night and remember that you are alone. It's a long time to accept dinner invitations from friends, knowing you will create an odd number at the table. It's a very long time to go without being kissed or told you are beautiful by a man who loves you. It's a long time to raise three children on your own, without a partner to lean on when things get tough or to celebrate with when things go well.

My mum is getting older, and I worry about her living alone. Will she remember to turn everything off before she goes to bed? Will she remember to lock the door at night? My sister, Frances, still lives in our town and stops by to see Mum every day. I'm glad she can be there, when I live so far away.

I thought about Mum a lot last week when I lost my wedding ring. Don't ask me why, but I tend to be careless with jewelry and car keys, and can never seem to remember where I put things. Mostly I call such items "misplaced," rather than "lost," because sooner or later they seem to show up again, in the strangest of places.

But not this time.

I remember putting my ring beside the coffee maker. I recall Barry moving it to the other side of the kitchen on top of some papers. And then . . . it vanished. Our best guess is that it went out with the trash.

I've felt so upset about it. How could I have been so careless? And then I thought about my mum and realized this could never have happened to her. She has never taken off her ring since the day my father put it on her finger. Twenty years after Dad's death, a hospital matron told her that the ring had to come off before her gall bladder surgery.

Mum looked at her and said, "Then you'll have to cut it off my finger," because she had no intention of removing it. They covered it with tape!

My mum's life reminds me that some hurts and hardships can last for a long, long time, but that faith and love can continue to endure even in the darkness. Her experience echoes that of many others through the centuries. I think in particular of two famous Teresas. They are famous to many, but sadly, they have often been missed by those whose only experience is of traditional Protestant churches. I was raised in Scotland, where a great divide exists between the Protestant and Roman Catholic churches. This mistrust goes back into our dark religious history and blinds us to what God continues to do in the lives of those who love Him no matter what label they wear. I first met these two women when I was a student in seminary, and their journeys—particularly the parts less publicized—have enriched my life. I pray they will enrich your life too.

Mother Teresa: Faith and Doubt

The world knows Agnes Bojaxhiu as Mother Teresa, a Roman Catholic nun who founded an order called The Missionaries of Charity in Calcutta, India. The world remembers her as a selfless advocate for the poor and as the 1979 winner of the Nobel Peace Prize.

But usually it remembers only part of her story.

By the age of twelve, Teresa believed that God had called her to become a missionary to spread the love of Christ. At age eighteen, she joined the Sisters of Loreto, and from 1931 to 1948 she taught at St. Mary's High School in Calcutta. But in response to the deplorable conditions she saw in the slums there, she left her position at the school to begin ministering to the poorest of the poor. Over the years, thousands of young women joined her work, and today the order has major outreaches not only in India but in Asia, Africa, and Latin America, as well as houses in North America, Europe, and Australia, where it ministers to shut-ins, alcoholics, the homeless, and people suffering from AIDS.

In August 2007—about ten years after her death on September 5, 1997—a book titled *Mother Teresa: Come Be My Light* hit store shelves, causing something of a sensation. The book published a collection of Teresa's private correspondence with her "confessors" and superiors over a period of sixty-six years, revealing a Teresa hardly anyone knew. The book created such a stir that *Time* magazine carried a lengthy article describing both the book and the public reaction to it, called "Mother Teresa's Crisis of Faith."[15]

Teresa never wanted anyone to read her letters; she requested that they be destroyed upon her death. But her church overruled her, and the book reveals a woman of faith who for almost fifty years struggled to sense God's presence—*any* presence at all. Her correspondence makes frequent reference to her "dryness," "darkness," "loneliness," and even "torture." To one spiritual advisor, she wrote, "I spoke as if my very heart was in love with God—tender, personal love. If you were [there], you would have said, 'What hypocrisy.'" One undated note, addressed to Jesus and written at the behest of a confessor, said this:

> Lord, my God, who am I that You should forsake me? The Child of your Love—and now become as the most hated one—the one—You have thrown away as unwanted—unloved. I call, I cling, I want—and there is no One to answer—no One on Whom I can cling—no, No One.—Alone . . . . Where is my Faith—even deep down right in there is nothing, but emptiness & darkness—My God—how painful is this unknown pain—I have no Faith—I dare not utter the words & thoughts that crowd in my heart—& make me suffer untold agony.
>
> So many unanswered questions live within me afraid to uncover them—because of the blasphemy—If there be God—please forgive me—When I try to raise my thoughts to Heaven—there is such convicting emptiness that those very thoughts return like sharp knives & hurt my very soul.—I am told God loves me—and yet the reality of darkness & cold-ness & emptiness is so great that nothing touches my soul.

Such desperate words—and many, many more like them—stunned a world that had grown used to Mother Teresa saying very different things in public, as she did one year as Christmas approached. At that time she said the holiday should remind everyone that "radiating joy is real" because Christ is everywhere, "in our hearts, Christ is in the poor we meet, Christ in the smile we give and in the smile that we receive."

Most people never imagined that Teresa could also write in private, "Such deep longing for God—and . . . repulsed—empty—no faith—no love—no zeal . . . . Heaven means nothing—pray for me please that I keep smiling at Him in spite of everything."

So was Teresa a hypocrite? Did she say one thing in public but believe something very different in private? Or does she picture for us (in an extreme form) the "dark nights of the soul" that many saints have described and written about for centuries? In 1951, Teresa wrote about Jesus and His passion, "I want to . . . drink ONLY from His chalice of pain," and it appears that the Lord answered her prayer in a way she did not expect, perhaps giving her excruciating insight into one of the apostle Paul's more mysterious sayings: "I rejoice in what was suffered for you, and I fill up in my flesh what is still lacking in regard to Christ's afflictions, for the sake of his body, which is the church" (Colossians 1:24).

One of Teresa's spiritual advisors, Rev. Joseph Neuner, gave the troubled woman some counsel that appears to have greatly helped her. He told her three things. First, no human remedy existed for her condition, and so she should not feel guilty for her feelings. Second, "feeling Jesus" was not the only proof of His presence, and her longing for God provided a "sure sign" of Christ's "hidden presence" in her life. And third, Jesus' perceived absence was in fact an important part of the "spiritual side" of her work.

Neuner later called it "the redeeming experience of her life" when Teresa "realized that the night of her heart was the special share she had in Jesus' passion." Teresa must have agreed, because she wrote back to Neuner, "I can't express in words—the gratitude I owe you for your kindness to me— for the first time in . . . years—I have come to love the darkness."

Toward the end of his article, the writer of the *Time* story expressed his opinion that if Teresa "could carry on for a half century without God in her head or heart, then perhaps people not quite as saintly can cope with less extreme versions of the same problem." And Rev. Brian Kolodiejchuk, the compiler and editor of *Mother Teresa: Come Be My Light*, hoped the book might help to counter a problem we've already mentioned: "The tendency in our spiritual life but also in our more general attitude toward love is that our feelings are all that is going on. And so to us the totality of love is what we feel. But to really love someone requires commitment, fidelity and vulnerability. Mother Teresa wasn't 'feeling' Christ's love, and she could have shut down. But she was up at 4:30 every morning for Jesus, and still writing to him, 'Your happiness is all I want.'"

Now, since you've made it this far in this book, I suspect you know something of what it means to suffer through a "dark night of the soul." Very often, that night can last much longer than the few hours the sun disappears every day. For some of us, that night can last days, weeks, months, and in some cases (like Teresa's), decades.

I pray that your "dark night" doesn't stretch to such extreme lengths.

I pray that the dawn comes soon—the merest hint of gray on the eastern horizon that blossoms into a lovely new sunrise in your life.

But if the darkness should linger, I also pray that you would ponder another of the apostle Paul's less-celebrated statements: "For it has been granted to you on behalf of Christ not only to believe on him, but also to suffer for him, since you are going through the same struggle you saw I had, and now hear that I still have" (Philippians 1:29–30).

I would also ask you to consider the last days of John the Baptist, after King Herod arrested him and put him on death row. As John sat in the stinking, dark hole of Herod's prison, doubts rose up to trouble and harass him. Had it all been for nothing? Was Jesus really who he'd thought He was? Had he miscalculated? In the darkness of his tiny cell, John began to doubt his mission, his faith, and his own judgment. So he sent some of his followers to ask Jesus, "Are you the one who was to come, or should we expect someone else?" (Matthew 11:3). Remember, this is the very same John who earlier shouted to the crowds about Jesus, "Look, the Lamb of God, who takes away the sin of the world!" (John 1:29).

Prolonged suffering had made John ripe for second-guessing. Perhaps he expected the Messiah to break him out of his cell and usher in the long-awaited kingdom. But day after day, there he sat, in the dark and in the dirt, while an evil king continued to party.

Do you recall how Jesus responded? He didn't send someone to rebuke John: "I'm so disappointed in you, John! People of faith don't talk like that. Shame on you! No wonder you're still in prison. If you had a little more faith, then maybe I'd see about getting you out of there." But neither did Jesus send John a direct answer to his anguished question: "Yes, dear cousin, I really am the Messiah. You can take it to the bank. I am the prophesied Savior of Israel!"

Instead, he told John's men, "Go back and report to John what you hear and see: The blind receive sight, the lame walk, those who have leprosy are cured, the deaf hear, the dead are raised, and the good news is preached to the poor" (Matthew 11:4–5). In other words, "Guys, you've seen the miracles and works I'm doing. John knows very well that these things were meant as signs to point Israel to the true Messiah. You know that none of the prophets ever healed a blind man—but many blind men have received their sight through Me."

And then Jesus said one final, intriguing thing: "Blessed is the man who does not fall away on account of me" (Matthew 11:6). This single sentence amounted to a gentle admonition from the Good Shepherd: "John, I know you're discouraged. I know life hasn't turned out like you thought it would. I know I haven't done for you what you hoped I would. But even in that dreary prison cell, and even with the executioner's sword poised over your head, I want you to know that you are a blessed man. I know it doesn't *feel* like that. I know it doesn't *look* like that. But don't give up your faith in Me, John! Don't give up now. Just a few more steps—and then you'll know it was all worth it all." And perhaps the most poignant question of all: "John, will you still love a God you don't understand?"

A life of faith does not mean a life without pain.

But neither does a pain-filled life of faith mean a life without sunshine! Teresa of Avila makes that equally valid point.

Teresa of Avila: Difficulty and Delight

Although she lived some four and a half centuries ago, the writings and exploits of Teresa of Avila continue to inspire people today. When I think of Teresa, I always think of one of her shorter prayers and one of her even shorter commentaries. I'll give you the commentary first.

This woman who became St. Teresa was born in 1515 to wealthy, prominent Spanish parents. She lost her mother at an early age and at sixteen was sent away to a boarding school. Teresa suffered from poor health during her later teen years, but also at that time determined to become a nun, in 1536 joining the Convent of the Incarnation as a novice and taking her vows a few months later as a Carmelite. Her illnesses continued, however, and she suffered a period of paralysis. By 1542, she had recovered physically, but spiritually her health had declined. She later said she grew spiritually luke-warm, gave up the practice of "mental prayer," and admitted, "Very often, over a period of several years, I was more occupied in wishing my hour of prayer were over, and in listening whenever the clock struck, than in thinking of things which were good. Again and again I would rather have done any severe penance" than prepare for prayer.[16]

When the Jesuits came to Avila in 1555, Teresa confessed to Father Juan de Padranos that she had seen a life-changing vision of the wounded Christ. "This was the beginning of Teresa's mystical life," wrote Clayton Berg, but "it also represented the beginning of opposition from her confessors and other friends who pronounced her to be possessed." Even after her teaching and practice received official approval from the church, the Inquisition caused her serious problems; nevertheless, she went on to write several classic books on prayer and devotion, and founded seventeen convents or foundations.

It is said that one day as Teresa attempted to mount a donkey for a trip, she fell off the beast and into a mud puddle. Reportedly she looked up to heaven and said to God, "If this is how You treat Your friends, no wonder You have so few of them."

The prayer I have in mind has a similar quality. She once prayed, "From silly devotions and sour-faced saints, spare us, O Lord."

Amen! I love this woman!

Teresa wrote using simple but potent images, the best known of which is perhaps the one represented in her classic work, *Interior Castle*. She used the image of a Castle, as a picture of the wholeness of the soul. In the Castle the whole person experiences God through His indwelling presence. Teresa saw almost infinite possibilities for a person to experience the majesty of God within the solitary, interior life.

Teresa had almost no formal education, and yet her church continually instructed her to write. She often did not feel up to the task. In the introduction to her *Interior Castle*, written sometime after she had passed her sixtieth birthday, she wrote:

> Few tasks which I have been commanded to undertake by obedience have been so difficult as this present one of writing about matters relating to prayer: for one reason, because I do not feel that the Lord has given me either the spirituality or the desire for it . . . . Their [her fellow Carmelite nuns] only excuse for crediting me with it [that is, the ability to solve problems in prayer] could be their having as little understanding as I have ability in these matters.[17]

Such unfeigned humility continued right up to her deathbed, when she spoke her last words over and over again. Those words came from Psalm 51:17, which says, "The sacrifices of God are a broken spirit: a broken and contrite heart, O God, thou wilt not despise" (KJV). Clayton Berg therefore could rightly say that the "hard core of Santa Teresa's 'spiritual virility'" is found in these words from her *Life*: "Come what may the great thing to do is for us to embrace the cross."

A Teresa Named Naomi

How do you respond to these two Teresas, separated by centuries but united in their devotion to Christ, regardless of their hardships, challenges, and disappointments? Neither had an easy life, and both left this world focused on the cross of Christ—an instrument of torture and death that nevertheless brings us life.

Right now, at this moment, in your own hardships and disappointments, what do you think of these two women? Do they encourage you? Worry you? Inspire you? Frighten you?

For me, they not only point the way to finding hope when hope seems lost, but they also remind me of another woman, thousands of years before either of them, who faced and finally overcame her own set of horrible circumstances. Together, these women (along with my mum) encourage me to keep pressing on.

I'm thinking of Naomi, the mother-in-law of Ruth (for whom the brief Old Testament book of Ruth is named). A famine prompted Naomi, her husband, and their two sons to leave Israel for a foreign country; and there, in that pagan land, Naomi lost all three of them. The men in her life all died, one after another, leaving her alone, destitute, and far from home.

It was more than Naomi could bear. Not only did her heart break, but her faith shattered too. Listen to the anguish in her voice as she said to her widowed daughters-in-law: "Things are far more bitter for me than for you, because the LORD himself has raised his fist against me" (Ruth 1:13 NLT).

And she told them, "Do not call me Naomi [pleasant]; call me Mara [bitter], for the Almighty has dealt very bitterly with me. I went away full, and the LORD has brought me back empty. Why call me Naomi, when the LORD has testified against me and the Almighty has brought calamity upon me?" (Ruth 1:20–21 ESV).

If ever there were a broken, disappointed woman, it was Naomi. Nothing made sense to her anymore. She had left her home in Bethlehem full of heart and young in years, and now she was returning empty and old. Everything she had been brought up to believe, she left buried with her husband and two sons in a foreign country. So she determined to return to Bethlehem, to live out her remaining days a shattered and miserable woman.

Do you recognize her story in your own? Yes, the circumstances will differ; I realize that. But the devastating disillusionment is the same. Everything you have believed and held on to your whole life lies in ashes at your feet, and nothing makes sense anymore. I remember talking to a woman who had buried three children. Etched into every line around her eyes, I saw her raw pain.

"I don't pray anymore," she told me. "Why would I? My prayers, my tears, my begging made no difference to God."

That's just how Naomi felt, betrayed and abandoned by God.

Is that how you feel? Have circumstances taken such a sharp turn that you wonder if God still sees you? Do you question why God seems to answer the prayers of other women, but somehow it's as though He can't hear you—or has turned away from you? (Mother Teresa once wrote to a spiritual confidant, "Jesus has a very special love for you, [but] as for me, the silence and the emptiness is so great, that I look and do not see,—Listen and do not hear—the tongue moves [in prayer] but does not speak.") Do you ever feel as if the circumstances of your life speak of God's disapproval of who you are?

What Naomi could not know was that regardless of all outward appearances, regardless of her heartbreaking circumstances, regardless of how things seemed or felt to her, God had not abandoned her. He had not forsaken her. As her weary feet shuffled into Bethlehem, her homecoming would be nothing at all like she had imagined. Desolation would not follow desolation, as her heart told her it would. The gifts of family, home, children, and enduring love would soon overtake her and fill the rest of her life with contentment. She would be surprised by joy.

But she couldn't have known that on the long road home. She couldn't have realized how God had been at work behind the scenes, orchestrating events that would bring Naomi the peace and joy and overflowing heart she couldn't have imagined at the time. He *was* answering her prayers, just not the way she expected.

Even if she couldn't see it.

Even if she didn't believe it.

If you know her story, you remember that it has the most spectacularly happy ending. Through a series of miraculous events and divine coincidences, Naomi's daughter-in-law Ruth meets and falls in love with Boaz, a relative of Naomi's. Boaz willingly becomes Ruth's "kinsman-redeemer," carrying on the family's name and restoring their property rights and place in society by marrying the widow. Not only was Ruth loved and cared for, but Naomi was taken care of for the rest of her life. It's not only one of the greatest love stories of all time (if you haven't read it, please do!); it's also a beautiful picture of the love of Christ—our Kinsman-Redeemer—and all He has done for us, His Bride. In fact, with the birth of their son, Obed, Boaz and Ruth become part of the lineage of Christ—ancestors in His family tree.

So many things in Naomi's story speak to me. First, God had remained faithful to Naomi, regardless of whether she saw it or felt it or believed it. *Her lack of faith didn't keep Him from showing her kindness and grace.* It didn't keep Him from fulfilling His plans for her. Our patient God had compassion on her. He didn't punish her or strike her dead for the accusations she brought against Him or the faithless things she said. As her great-great-grandson David would one day write, "He does not treat us as our sins deserve" (Psalm 103:10).

Naomi's bitterness blinded her to the ongoing gift of God's presence, His peace, and His comfort in the midst of her trials. She allowed her misery to drown out the tender, compassionate voice of God. But still, joy—and grandchildren—came to her in the end: "Then the women said to Naomi, 'Praise the LORD, who has not left you without a family redeemer today. May his name became well known in Israel. He will renew your life and sustain you in your old age. Indeed, your daughter-in-law, who loves you and is better to you than seven sons, has given birth to him.' Naomi took the child, placed him on her lap, and took care of him" (Ruth 4:14–16 HCSB).

That baby grew up to be the father of Jesse, who grew up to be the father of David, the most celebrated king in Israel's history and the man whom all the people thought of centuries later when they called Jesus "the Son of David."

Turning Point

How are you responding to the brokenness in your own life? Do you find yourself at a crossroads, a turning point? Maybe it's time you made a choice, a declaration, that God is God—*your* God—and there is no turning back for you. Ruth made this choice in the darkest moment of her life. I think the most profound, life-changing spiritual decisions are almost always made in the dark.

I have stood on that road as well. Perhaps for the first time you want to join the millions down through the centuries who have decided to choose God in the midst of our brokenness, in the midst of our suffering and pain. Together—my mum, the Teresas, Ruth, and countless others—say, "God, You are my God. I will follow You and I will not turn back, for there is nothing else for me in this life. No life, apart from You!"

This, too, is a gift of brokenness. It reveals to us the only real choice, the only true choice, we have.

A German pastor named Dietrich Bonhoeffer made that choice more than sixty years ago. A lifelong pacifist, he decided in the middle of World War II that he needed to do what he could to rid his beloved homeland, and the world, of the evil of Adolf Hitler. He joined a conspiracy to assassinate Hitler, and when the attempt failed, he and others who took part in the plan were arrested and imprisoned. The Nazis hung him (using piano wire) just days before the Allies liberated the camp where he had been held captive.

Sometime during his imprisonment Bonhoeffer penned a poem titled "Who Am I?" Although he struggled to know himself, he had a firm grip on the most important element of his true identity. If you can make the last line your own, then you, too, can make it through your difficulties, whatever they may be.

"WHO AM I?"

Who am I? They often tell me
I stepped from my cell's confinement
Calmly, cheerfully, firmly,
Like a squire from his country-house.
Who am I? They often tell me
I used to speak to my warders
Freely and friendly and clearly,
As though it were mine to command.
Who am I? They also tell me
I bore the days of misfortune
Equally, smilingly, proudly,
Like one accustomed to win.

Am I really all that which other men tell of?
Or am I only what I myself know of myself?
Restless and longing and sick, like a bird in a cage,
Struggling for breath, as though hands were
Compressing my throat,
Yearning for colors, for flowers, for the voices of birds,
Thirsting for words of kindness, for neighborliness,
Tossing in expectation of great events,
Powerlessly trembling for friends at an infinite distance,
Weary and empty at praying, at thinking, at making,
Faint, and ready to say farewell to it all?

Who am I? This or the other?
Am I one person today and tomorrow another?
Am I both at once? A hypocrite before others,
And before myself a contemptibly woebegone weakling?
Or is something within me still like a beaten army,
Fleeing in disorder from victory already achieved?
Who am I? They mock me, these lonely questions of mine.
Whoever I am, Thou knowest, O God, I am Thine!

Eight

Fierce Love and Halloween Grace

Why God's Ferocious Commitment to You Comes with Surprises

According to a traditional folk tale, once there were three little trees, all with big dreams. The first tree dreamed of being carved into a beautiful and ornate treasure box that would hold the greatest treasure the world had ever seen. The second tree dreamed of being fashioned into a great ship that would sail the Seven Seas. The third tree didn't want to leave its home on the mountaintop. "I want to grow so tall that when people stop to look at me," he said, "they'll raise their eyes to heaven and think of God."

One day when the young saplings had grown into tall, strong trees, three woodcutters climbed the mountain. As they cut down the first tree, it could barely contain its excitement—it just knew it would soon fulfill its destiny. But instead of an elaborate treasure chest, workers made the tree into a plain, ordinary feedbox for farm animals. The tree felt bitterly disappointed.

The second tree got made into a ship, all right—but not the kind to crest the waves of mighty oceans. It became just a simple fishing vessel, floating in a lake—not the stuff dreams are made of.

The third tree, to its horror and dismay, also got chopped down, cut into wooden beams, and then left to gather dust in a lumberyard. "All I ever wanted was to stay on the mountaintop and point to God," it moaned.

Time passed and the trees forgot their dreams, until one night when a young woman placed her baby in the animal feedbox—and the first tree knew that indeed it carried the greatest treasure on earth.

Another night, a tired man and his friends crowded onto the little fishing boat. They got halfway across the lake when a terrible storm blew in, threatening to tear the boat to pieces. The tired man stood up and said, "Peace, be still." The second tree knew then that it was carrying the King of heaven and earth.

One Friday morning the third tree felt itself yanked from the woodpile and dragged through city streets, where crowds shouted insults. The tree felt cruel and ugly when it realized it had become an instrument of torture. Soldiers nailed a man's hands and feet to its beams. But on Sunday morning, when the sun rose and the earth trembled with joy, the tree stood tall, knowing that from now on, it would forever point people to God.

I love that simple story because it reminds me that God has good plans for us *that we simply can't envision*. Our experience of life, and what we hope to experience from life, sometimes live so far apart from each other that the yawning distance prompts us to doubt God's love and grace.

Remember Naomi in the last chapter? She had already renamed herself *Mara*—Bitter—believing that nothing could redeem her life, nothing could redeem her hope, purpose, and joy.

That was before a certain kinsman-redeemer stepped into her life . . . and changed everything.

Somehow we really believe that love means giving us what we imagine we want, and grace means never getting what we don't want. As a result, we conclude that if we don't get what we want but do get what we never wanted, then God must not really love us, and His grace must not really cover us.

Do you and I, then, misunderstand or perhaps misjudge what God is all about in our lives?

Of course we do.

Beyond Unconditional Love

Our generation has grown up on the idea of the "unconditional love of God." Although the phrase never appears in Scripture, it almost seems that one can't speak of "the love of God" today without adding the "unconditional" part. The idea might not be inspired, but it certainly has become entrenched.

I'm pretty sure I understand why we use the phrase and why it has become so popular. The phrase really is trying to get at a crucial, even foundational biblical truth: namely, that when God sets His love upon us and adopts us into His own family, His love remains upon us regardless of what might happen and regardless of what we might do. He loves us with an eternal love, and "eternal" means His love doesn't wax and wane as ours so often does. His love *remains*.

We see this incomparable truth played out time and again in the Scriptures, in both Testaments.

- Abraham, the "man of faith," lies about his wife to save his own skin (not once, but twice, and many years apart), and yet God makes him into a great nation through whom the Messiah comes.
- Moses kills a man and disobeys God publicly before all Israel, and yet thousands of years later shows up with Elijah at the Transfiguration, encouraging Jesus before His own imminent trial.
- David commits adultery and tries to cover it up with a murder, and yet God still loves him and continues to protect his family line until the appearance of Jesus, "the Son of David."
- Peter denies the Lord three times, yet still God taps him to help lead Christ's church.

Look sometime into the people mentioned in the "Hall of Faith" in Hebrews 11, and see how many of them had less-than-stellar records. (Jephthah gets a Hebrews 11 gold star? Really? *Jephthah?* The man who made a rash and foolish oath that doomed his joyful, loving daughter? Read his story in Judges 11.) This is all nothing but great news for broken people!

And that's exactly why I don't think "unconditional" does God's love justice.

I worry that by constantly using the phrase—and seldom explaining what we mean by it—we've robbed it of its original force. People today hear it and tend to think that when they sin against the Lord, He'll respond, "It's okay; don't worry about it. I'll love you anyway," when I think He really responds with something more like, "I'll love you forever, and that's why it's *not* okay."

For me, the reason why I use the term *unconditional love* less and less these days comes down to its bloodless, passionless tone. The word *unconditional* feels so cold to me, so distant, so clinical, and devoid of emotion. It sounds to me like a mere legal designation. Imagine that a long-incarcerated prisoner finally wins his unconditional release from jail. We know the former prisoner celebrates; we can see it in our mind's eye. But what about the warden? I get no mental picture of him singing or dancing for joy; more likely, he has a bored or even dour expression on his face as he mechanically signs the legally required release papers. He has nothing emotionally invested in the prisoner's release. He's just doing his job.

That is *not* a picture of the love of God for broken people! Our God loves with passion, with fire, with bone-rattling force. His furious emotion would consume us if His love did not shield us from its full intensity.

Years ago I remember reading about a man who left a church for a surprising reason. We read it in Brennan Manning's *Ragamuffin Gospel*. Listen to how the man rejected "the pastel-colored patsy God who promises to never rain on our parade":

A pastor I know recalls a Sunday morning Bible study at his church when the text under consideration was Genesis 22. In this passage, God commands Abraham to take his son Isaac and offer him in sacrifice on Mount Moriah. After the group read the passage, the pastor offered some historical background on this period in salvation history, including the prevalence of child sacrifice among the Canaanites. The group listened in awkward silence.

Then the pastor asked, "But what does this story mean to *us*?"

A middle-aged man spoke up. "I'll tell you the meaning this story has for me. I've decided that me and my family are looking for another church."

The pastor was astonished. "What? Why?"

"Because," the man said, "when I look at that God, the God of Abraham, I feel I'm near a *real* God, not the sort of dignified, businesslike, Rotary Club God we chatter about here on Sunday mornings. Abraham's God could blow a man to bits, give and then take a child, ask for everything from a person, and then want more. I want to know *that* God."

And then Manning wrote,

The child of God knows that the graced life calls him or her to live on a cold and windy mountain, not on the flattened plain of reasonable, middle-of-the-road religion.

For at the heart of the gospel of grace, the sky darkens, the wind howls, a young man walks up another Moriah in obedience to a God who demands everything and stops at nothing. Unlike Abraham, he carries a cross on his back rather than sticks for the fire . . . like Abraham, listening to a wild and restless God who will have His way with us, no matter what the cost. [18]

God's love for us is not merely "unconditional," but wild, windy, even howling. It demands everything. It stops at nothing. In a word, it is *fierce*.

I am reminded of a famous passage in *The Lion, the Witch and the Wardrobe* where C. S. Lewis introduces us to Aslan, a great Lion who pictures Jesus Christ Himself. Before the story's young protagonists meet Aslan for the first time, they ask to hear about him from some talking animals who live in the enchanted land of Narnia. Listen to their conversation (Mr. Beaver starts first):

"Don't you know who is the King of Beasts? Aslan is a lion—*the* Lion, the great Lion."

"Ooh!" said Susan, "I'd thought he was a man. Is he—quite safe? I shall feel rather nervous about meeting a lion."

"That you will, dearie, and no mistake," said Mrs. Beaver, "if there's anyone who can appear before Aslan without their knees knocking, they're either braver than most or else just silly."

"Then he isn't safe?" said Lucy.

"Safe?" said Mr. Beaver. "Don't you hear what Mrs. Beaver tells you? Who said anything about safe? 'Course he isn't safe. But he's good. He's the King, I tell you."[19]

Toward the end of the book, after Aslan saves Narnia from an evil witch and puts right everything that had gone terribly wrong, the great Lion simply slips away. Men and beasts look about for him, but he has vanished. Lewis then has his young heroes recall an earlier speech by Mr. Beaver about Aslan: "He'll be coming and going. One day you'll see him and another you won't. He doesn't like being tied down—and of course he has other countries to attend to. It's quite all right. He'll often drop in. Only you mustn't press him. He's wild, you know. Not like a *tame* lion."[20]

Many of us love to recall these memorable scenes and even reflect on how Jesus—our Aslan—is neither safe nor tame. But then when hardship rips through our lives like a Texas tornado, and we can't seem to see Jesus in its devastating wake, our spirits sink. We wonder where He is, why He seems to hide Himself, and if He really loves us after all. And maybe we begin to wish His "wildness" were a bit more . . . well, safe. And to hear of God's "unconditional love" in those circumstances, in my experience, helps very little.

But what if we saw His love as *fierce*?

Blogger Richard J. Vincent has written that God's "kind, gentle love is not the sentimental, sappy variety. . . . Instead, this love is strong. This love is a fierce love, a positive force that conquers sin, evil, and death. It is the burning passion to overcome evil with good. It is a steadfast commitment to the good of another—even if that other is one's enemy. It is a love that does not put self or stuff at the center of life, but gives itself away with joyful abandon. It is a love so secure in another that it loses its life for others, only to find its life again."[21]

Take another look at that most famous of Bible verses, John 3:16.

If any verse seems "safe," it has to be this one. Isn't this the verse little children are taught before they're even sure of their ABCs?

Those of us with any Christian background at all know this passage so well and quote it so much that it might as well be encased in plastic. It's safe and familiar as a favorite bathrobe or an old pair of slippers. As a result, we tend to forget the depth of the divine passion it reflects.

"For God so loved the world," John wrote, *"that he gave his one and only son."*

Stop there for a moment. Just how did God "give" this only Son of His? He gave Him, not as a shiny new present under the tree, but as a helpless human baby who arrived on earth to die. God gave Jesus to us, knowing that we would spit on Him, slap Him, mock Him, tear out His beard, rip open His back with jagged bits of bone and metal, smash a crown of thorns into His scalp, nail Him to a tree, and thrust a spear into His dead body. This is not "unconditional" love; this is fierce love, written in towering letters beyond our ability to fully read or comprehend.

If you still doubt the magnitude of God's passionate, fiery love, then read again what He thinks of those who dismiss the lengths He went to in order to save us:

> Anyone who refused to obey the law of Moses was put to death without mercy on the testimony of two or three witnesses. Just think how much more terrible the punishment will be for those who have trampled on the Son of God, and have treated the blood of the covenant, which made us holy, as if it were common and unholy, and have insulted and disdained the Holy Spirit who brings God's mercy to us.
>
> For we know the one who said,
> "I will take revenge.

I will pay them back."

He also said,

"The LORD will judge his own people."

It is a terrible thing to fall into the hands of the living God.

(Hebrews 10:28–31 NLT)

This is no passage to take lightly. These are not words reflecting a distant, unfeeling deity. The passage instead echoes the heart of a God who fiercely loves His own—and who will go to staggering lengths to shape them into people who resemble His own dear Son.

All of this leads us to a very difficult question.

And here it is: do we imagine that the living God—the One whom the writer of Hebrews later calls "a consuming fire"—loves His only Son *less* than He loves us?

No, you say, of course not.

But if God loves His Son beyond anything we can possibly conceive, and yet His fierce love moved Him to sacrifice that beloved Son on our behalf—then what does that imply for *us*? What might that same fierce love ask *us* to do, in order to broadcast to the world and to angels that God Himself is the greatest treasure of all? Can we say with finality that the pain, trial, hardship, difficulty, or tragedy that we face is simply over the top and too much . . . and therefore must mean that God doesn't *really* love us?

The cross shouts, "No!"

The truth is, we simply cannot know at any particular moment what God ultimately is up to in our lives, any more than the three trees of the old fable knew.

Can things get bad?

Yes.

Can they get worse?

Yes.

Does that mean God's fierce love for us has vanished?

No, no, no.

Author and teacher Steve Brown knows all about this. He has an amazing sense of humor and, I think, a keen grasp of God's fierce love. In his book *A Scandalous Freedom*, Steve ends a chapter called "The Pain We Avoid . . . and the Reality That Sets Us Free" with a story about loss. Although he tells it in his typical wry way, he draws an important application.

Steve describes how he survived 1992's Hurricane Andrew, one of the most destructive storms in U.S. history. He and his wife tried to wait out the hurricane in their home, but like nearly everyone else, they didn't realize the power of this raging monster. Although they had done everything they could, he admits, "It wasn't nearly enough."

As Steve and his wife crouched in their bedroom closet, they realized they might die. They heard trees crash into their home, the roof blow off, and finally the house around them fall apart. "That was really bad," Steve wrote, "but there's more."

After they lost many of their possessions in the hurricane, a dishonest contractor stole about $60,000 from them, and other contractors put liens of $15,000 on what was left of their home—$75,000 they didn't have. "That was really bad," Steve wrote, "but there's more."

In the interim they stayed in a small apartment, and one day when Steve went out to the parking lot, he discovered someone had stolen his car. "That was really bad," Steve wrote, "but there's more." (Do you sense a pattern here?)

About that time doctors told Steve that his mother had only a short time to live. Since the Browns no longer had a house, they couldn't bring her there, so they moved to his mother's old homestead in the mountains of North Carolina to nurse his mum until her death. Steve took a small recorder and prepared his daily radio broadcast from the back porch of his mother's aging home.

To that point in his life, Steve said, he'd enjoyed a fairly easy life and never had to face a devastating tragedy. Although he sometimes preached on pain and suffering, he sensed his words had a hollow ring. Although Steve called the whole complex of events "a horrible experience," he called it "wonderful too." His Christian mother got to say good-bye to friends and family, give her grandchildren advice, pray a lot, and even tell jokes. "Oh yes," he wrote, "there were tears, pain, and fear."

But in the middle of all this tragedy, God came. And in facing it all, we discovered a boundless and exhilarating freedom and joy we had never known.

It wasn't the freedom of the Christian who pretends that things are all right when they're not. It was the freedom that only believers who have faced pain and tragedy know. It was the freedom of Jesus who, when we've lost it all, invites us to laugh, dance, and sing in his presence, knowing that nothing will ever separate us from him and his love.

That's good enough. But then Steve adds one final pearl of wisdom: "Pain is not something most people like. That is why we run from it as fast as we can. That is also why we aren't free. Jesus hardly ever goes to those places where we run."[22]

Are you running? Does the pain have you fleeing to . . . who knows where? I can't explain why God has allowed this difficult thing into your life. I'm not sure it would help you if I did know and I told you.

But what I do know is this: God loves you with a ferocity that defies description. It's no sugarcoated love. It's not a romantic, head-over-heels kind of love. It's not even a so-called unconditional love. His love is *fierce*.

And that fierce love—a fiery love that burns at the very gates of Eden—will get you all the way home.

The Grace of the Flaming Sword

The last few verses of Genesis 3 have had a profound impact on my life. I used to read them as judgment, but now I see them as full of grace from a God who loves us fiercely. I titled this book *God Loves Broken People* because that is the theme of my life and the experience of my heart. I used to view brokenness as the bad news, but now because of the outrageous grace of God, I see it as a profound, breathtaking gift. And Genesis 3:22–24 (ESV) shows me its truth:

> Then the LORD God said, "Behold, the man has become like one of us in knowing good and evil. Now, lest he reach out his hand and take also of the tree of life and eat, and live forever—" therefore the LORD God sent him out from the garden of Eden to work the ground from which he was taken. He drove out the man, and at the east of the garden of Eden he placed the cherubim and a flaming sword that turned every way to guard the way to the tree of life.

Do you see grace in this passage?

"Well, Sheila," you might reply, "not exactly. How do this angelic sentry and a flaming sword show grace?"

Why would God put that sword there in the first place?

The answer is right there in the passage above: *"Now, lest he reach out his hand and take also of the tree of life and eat, and live forever . . ."*

Can you imagine what would have happened if God had allowed our fallen First Parents to stay in the garden and eat from the Tree of Life? Yes, they would have lived forever—but forever broken. Eternally miserable. Wracked with guilt. Fearful. And empty—oh, so very empty. Their eternal "life" would have become an eternal hell, full of guilt and shame and bitterness and regret. As the centuries and millennia rolled by, they would continue to hide from God and blame each other for their pain.

And then think of how they would feel to see their children, grandchildren, and great-great-great-great-grandchildren continue to follow their lead and fall into sin and depravity. It would be the tragedy of Cain and Abel a billion times over!

Physical death, a gift of grace? Oh my, yes! If you don't die, then how can you be born again?

I call this kind of grace "Halloween grace," because it wears an unanticipated costume. (You were wondering when I was going to explain that one, weren't you?) As I write, the calendar tells me that November 1, All Saints' Day, has arrived, which means that yesterday was October 31, Halloween. Last night kids all across America fanned out to knock on neighbors' doors, ring doorbells, shout "Trick or Treat!" and wait for candy to hit the bottom of their sacks. And pretty much all of those kids wore some kind of costume, from fairy princesses to superheroes. Now, I've noticed over the years that the costume on the outside doesn't necessarily give any clue to the sort of kid on the inside.

Grace can be like that too.

You see, God likes all kinds of grace. He doesn't go for one-size-fits-all grace. Remember how Peter spoke of "the manifold grace of God" (1 Peter 4:10 NASB)? Other versions translate the phrase, "God's grace in its various forms," "all these different graces of God" (JERUSALEM BIBLE), or "God's varied grace" (RSV). Some of these varied graces, we recognize immediately. At the beginning, His grace gave us justification from our sins (Romans 3:24).

Sometimes His grace gives us "eternal encouragement and good hope" (2 Thessalonians 2:16). At other times it instructs us to develop a proper, not an inflated, self-image (Romans 12:3). But in each case His grace wears a slightly different costume.

Remember this: not all grace looks like what we expected.

The apostle John said Jesus came to us from the Father, "full of grace and truth" (John 1:14). He didn't mean that sometimes Jesus had lots of grace, but little truth, and other times tons of truth, but not much grace. Jesus doesn't change like that any more than God does. What He is, He is *always*. So He always tells the truth. And He always comes with grace.

But the grace He brings can look *very* different from situation to situation!

Consider just a few of the statements Jesus made during His earthly ministry and note how different they sound from one another. Bear in mind, though, that in each case He spoke as a man "full of grace and truth."

- "It will be done just as you believed it would" (Matthew 8:13).
- "Let the dead bury their own dead" (Matthew 8:22).
- "Come to me, all you who are weary and burdened, and I will give you rest" (Matthew 11:28).
- "Are you still so dull?" (Matthew 15:16).
- "Blessed are you, Simon son of Jonah, for this was not revealed to you by man, but by my Father in heaven" (Matthew 16:17).
- "Get behind me, Satan! You are a stumbling block to me; you do not have in mind the things of God, but the things of men" (Matthew 16:23).

Does it seem to you that "Blessed are you" and "Get behind me, Satan" fit in the same grace category? To most of us, they don't *sound* equally gracious. Yet Jesus, the man John called "full of grace and truth," said both things to Peter. In fact, He made the second statement almost on the heels of the first. So it's not that the first was gracious, while the second wasn't. No, it's simply a matter of two differing situations needing two different kinds of grace. But it was grace all the same.

I've spent some time on this issue because broken people sometimes have trouble recognizing Halloween grace when it shows up. The costume throws them off. Or even frightens them. And so even with His grace right in front of their eyes, they imagine that God has run out of grace for them. I know how easy this is to do because I've done it myself.

More than once.

What does Halloween grace look like? I can't give you a description, because God has a very large costume closet. But I think I can give you a few biblical examples:

- When God put Jacob's hip out of joint and left him with a permanent, painful limp
- When an unspecified affliction helped the psalmist learn God's law
- When Jesus caused a minor panic among the disciples by telling them to feed a hungry crowd—without any provisions
- When three times the Lord refused Paul's request for healing, repeatedly telling the apostle he must keep his distressing "thorn in the flesh."[23]

I don't know what sort of Halloween grace the Lord might have working in your life right now. But if you have placed your faith in Jesus, then Jesus lives within you—which means that grace and truth live there too.

The trick is to look for the treats . . . and look beyond the costume.

A Different Dream

In our culture, we point to the best and brightest, as we see them: the rich, the powerful, the successful, the organized, the talented, the beautiful, the tan, the fit, the perfectly put-together. And yet our eyes see so very little.

If beauty, success, and money *really* brought happiness, then Hollywood, California, would be "the happiest place on earth" (not Disneyland). But we know it's not. The lives of the rich and famous often bear the scars of suicide, depression, drug and alcohol addiction, an almost desperate unhappiness, and the routine disintegration of relationships (as I write, one "celebrity marriage" has lasted a total of seventy-two days). These famous men and women may look glowing and glamorous on the pages of the tabloids, but the reality usually comes up far short of the fantasy.

So what is reality? Reality, for broken individuals like me, takes the form of 1 Peter 5:10. The apostle wrote, "And the God of all grace, who called you to his eternal glory in Christ, after you have suffered a little while, will himself restore you and make you strong, firm and steadfast." I don't normally quote long portions of commentaries, but William Barclay's insights into this verse shout encouragement to my heart. I think they will do the same for you. So read carefully what follows (and whenever Barclay declares what God wants to accomplish in a "man," recognize that the Lord wants to do this equally in a "woman"):

> Every one of the words which Peter uses has behind it a vivid picture. Each tells us something about what suffering is designed by God to do for a man.
>
> FIRST, through suffering God will *restore* a man.
>
> The word for *restore* is difficult in this case to translate. It is *Kartarizein*, the word commonly used for setting a fracture, the word used in Mark 1:19 for mending nets. It means to supply that which is missing, to mend that which is broken. So suffering, if accepted in humility and trust and love, can repair the weaknesses of a man's character and add the greatness which so far is not there. It is said that Sir Edward Elgar (beloved English composer best-known for his orchestral works including the *Enigma Variations*, the *Pomp and Circumstance Marches*) once listened to a young girl singing a solo from one of his own works. She had a voice of exceptional purity and clarity and range, and an almost perfect technique.
>
> When she had finished, Sir Edward said softly, "She will be really great when something happens to break her heart." J. M. Barrie (author of *Peter Pan*) tells how his mother lost her favorite son, and then says, "That is where my mother got her soft eyes, and that is why other mothers ran to her when they had lost a child." Suffering had done something for her that an easy way could never have done. Suffering is meant by God to add the grace notes to life.
>
> SECOND, through suffering God will *establish* a man.
>
> The word is *sterixein*, which means to make as solid as *granite*. Suffering of body and sorrow of heart do one of two things to man. They either make him collapse or they leave him with a solidity of character which he could never have gained anywhere else. If he meets them with continuing trust in Christ, he emerges like toughened steel that has been tempered in the fire.
>
> THIRD, through suffering God will *strengthen* a man.

The Greek is *sthenoun*, which means *to fill with strength*. Here is the same sense again. A life with no effort and no discipline almost inevitably becomes a flabby life. No one really knows what his faith means to him until it has been tried in the furnace of affliction. There is something doubly precious about a faith which has come victoriously through pain and sorrow and disappointment. The wind will extinguish a weak flame, but it will fan a strong flame into a still greater blaze. So it is with faith.

FINALLY, through suffering God will *settle* a man.

The Greek is *themelioun*, which means *to lay the foundations*. When we have to meet sorrow and suffering we are driven down to the very bedrock of faith. It is then that we discover what are the things which cannot be shaken. It is in time of trial that we discover the great truths on which real life is founded.[24]

God wants to take you to a place where darkness no longer feels quite so dark—but it never comes easily.

Behind the Curtain

Back in chapter 4, I wrote about Aaron and Holly McRae and their little girl, Kate, who suffered with a malignant brain tumor.

As I said, for more than a year after I'd encountered that devastating news on Twitter, I did nothing more than pray and write little notes in the guest book on her CaringBridge website.

When a short stay in their hometown of Phoenix came up in my travel schedule, however, I asked if I could meet them. Aaron wrote back and said they would love it, but as Kate was in Children's Hospital again, having yet another round of chemotherapy, I would have to visit them there.

As I took the elevator up to the Pediatric Oncology floor, everything within me screamed that such a place should not exist. Children should never be fed to such a ravenous beast. A staff nurse showed me how to scrub up, gave me a mask to wear, and showed me to Kate's room. I knocked gently on the door, and a young man answered. Aaron hugged me and invited me in.

Little Kate was fast asleep, hooked up to IV drips and monitors. She looked so tiny in the hospital bed. I had seen pictures of her before treatment, and all the beautiful locks of golden hair that once tumbled over her shoulders. Now it was gone.

Aaron told me that Holly had left to take a nap, but he would text her that I had arrived. I begged him to let her rest, but he said, "She would want to be here."

When Holly walked in, we hugged for a while. We talked. We laughed. We cried. We watched Kate.

Aaron, a pastor, expressed the chasm that exists for him at times between what he believes and what he sees. The fire he is walking through has burned away any easily won sentiment from his soul, but in its place there are a fierce love for Christ and a deep well of gratitude for the grace that they have all known.

Just as Toto tore away the drape revealing the Great Oz as nothing more than a scared little man, many of us feel disturbed when tragedy tears away the veneer of a comfortable faith. But it seems to me that when that drape disappears, we discover, unlike Dorothy and her traveling companions, that behind our pretty picture of a comfortable God roars a Lion whose fierce love burns with more intensity and magnificence than anything we ever could imagine.

NINE

NOTHING TO PROTECT, NOTHING TO LOSE

Three Choices When Suffering Move You from the Balcony to the Stage

There are many things in life over which we have no control. In the midst of unexpected circumstances, however, we encounter a mysterious and powerful friend-or-foe choice. The implications of some choices are minimal . . . will we have chicken or beef for dinner tonight? Some, however, have the power to change our destiny.

A recent issue of the *Dallas Morning News* carried a small but tragic story about murder, upbringing, and the choices we all make.

In late October, a man named Eric Franklin died when another man put a butcher knife through his throat. When police caught up to the suspect shortly after the killing, the man gave them his brother's name instead. The ruse didn't work, however, because police had just spoken to the suspect's brother.

His twin.

It turns out that while the forty-year-old suspect has a long list of prior criminal convictions, his twin has what police called "a spotless record."

How is this possible? How can a set of twins, raised in the same home, responding to the same parents, going to the same schools, playing with the same dog, eating the same breakfast cereal, and subjected to largely the same environment, turn out so very differently?

While I don't want to oversimplify the often complex factors that lead to such remarkable differences, I do want to focus on one factor that clearly plays a huge role.

Choice.

How we *choose* to respond to life's challenges, setbacks, and tragedies makes an enormous difference—not only to our own experience of life, but also to the experience of those who travel through life with us.

Choose!

Suffering and pain happen to all of us. They are as universal as rain in Seattle. But how we respond to that suffering and pain—what we choose in the midst of them—goes a long way toward determining the quality of our lives. As commentator William Barclay has written, "Suffering . . . may well drive a man to bitterness and despair; and may well take away such faith as he has. But if it is accepted in the trusting certainty that a father's hand will never cause his child a needless tear, then out of suffering come things which the easy way may never bring."[25]

God wants to bring rare, unexpected treasures out of *your* days of suffering, things that the easy way simply cannot bring.

I'm not talking about suffering itself, here. Of themselves, trials, heartaches, and hardships have no power to accomplish anything good in our lives. We all have witnessed how suffering can make a person (as the cliché would have it) bitter rather than better. The power of suffering to create beauty in your life lies almost entirely with you, in how you choose to react to the difficulties and even catastrophes that invade your life. In a sense, the angels hold their breath waiting to see how you will respond . . . and what you will choose.

Over and over in Scripture, God urges His people to choose their direction in life. That means there *is* a choice. He wouldn't ask us to choose unless we truly had real options before us. Listen to just a few of His instructions on choosing well:

- "I have set before you life and death, blessings and curses. *Now choose life*, so that you and your children may live and that you may love the LORD your God, listen to his voice, and hold fast to him" (Deuteronomy 30:19–20).
- "*Choose for yourselves this day whom you will serve*, whether the gods your forefathers served beyond the River, or the gods of the Amorites, in whose land you are living. But as for me and my household, we will serve the LORD" (Joshua 24:15).
- "Do not envy a violent man or *choose* any of his ways" (Proverbs 3:31).
- "How much better to get wisdom than gold, to *choose understanding* rather than silver!" (Proverbs 16:16).
- "For you have spent enough time in the past doing what pagans *choose*

to do—living in debauchery, lust, drunkenness, orgies, carousing and detestable idolatry" (1 Peter 4:3, emphasis added on passages above).

So how should we choose to respond to adversity and hardship? What choices can we make when life suddenly confronts us with options we neither like nor expect—nor ever anticipated? Again, Scripture overflows with good counsel here, but consider just a few of the choices we can make, regardless of the trials that elbow their way into our lives:

- "Let us not become weary in doing good, for at the proper time we will reap a harvest if we do not give up" (Galatians 6:9).
- "Let the peace of Christ rule in your hearts, since as members of one body you were called to peace. And be thankful" (Colossians 3:15).
- "Let us then approach the throne of grace with confidence, so that we may receive mercy and find grace to help us in our time of need" (Hebrews 4:16).
- "Let us hold unswervingly to the hope we profess, for he who promised is faithful" (Hebrews 10:23).
- "Through Jesus, therefore, let us continually offer to God a sacrifice of praise—the fruit of lips that confess his name" (Hebrews 13:15).

"Let us," of course, means we must *choose* to do all of these things.

Under normal conditions, in peaceful and pain-free broad daylight under a sunny blue sky, we may not struggle with making such decisions. But what about when storms close in and darkness descends? What then?

Then, perhaps, the choices don't come so easily.

Those who suffer from depression, for example, know that two of the things they need the most happen to be the very things they want the least. When depression settles on your heart like a cold, damp blanket, what you really want to do is go hide in your room and escape under the covers of your bed. What you don't want to do, what you feel you *cannot* do, is to reach out to others and go get some exercise.

When I feel the dank fog of depression wrap itself around me, I know that I have to fight it—with everything in me. But I never *want* to fight it. I want to surrender to it. I want to disappear in it, as I might disappear in the thick folds of a heavy fog on the moors. It always feels to me as if I've somehow lost my voice and am falling down and down into a well with no bottom.

Strange as it may seem, this is one of the reasons that I have dogs.

Not so with Tink. If it's time for her walk, Tink will stare at me. If I ignore her, she will bark. If I ignore that, she will bring her leash and drop it on my chest and sit with her nose two inches from mine. If I ignore that, she will tap me on the arm with her paw.

Tink doesn't really care if I'm struggling or troubled. Depression and melancholy? What is that to her? She has squirrels to chase and exciting scents to chase with her nose. For Tink's sake, then, not my own, I will drag myself out of bed, muttering things never uttered in the New Testament. But then, once I find myself outside in the fresh air under an open sky, I remember, "This too shall pass."

How we choose to respond to our dark times has more implications and consequences than I could possibly list, but in my experience, our suffering causes at least three major effects.

From the Balcony to the Stage

First, suffering moves us from the balcony to the stage. While we can learn some things about suffering from watching others go through it, persevering through our own suffering brings a whole new level of understanding (and even expertise).

Remember how in the last chapter we considered the various costumes that grace wears? God has many varieties of grace, two of which I have heard my friend Jennifer Rothschild call *spectator* grace and *participant* grace.

They are definitely not the same thing.

When the world of the patriarch Job fell apart, for example, he clearly benefited from participant grace. You simply can't go through what he did—the loss of all his children, his fortune, and finally his health—and still say things like, "The LORD gave and the LORD has taken away; may the name of the LORD be praised," and "Shall we accept good from God, and not trouble?" without a healthy dose of participant grace (see Job 1:21; 2:10).

When you suffer something as catastrophic as Job did, however, you also need a healthy dose of spectator grace filling your friends and family.

Here, however, Job came up a little short.

Major understatement!

Although his friends may have meant well (but I'm not even sure of

that), their words did far more harm than good. Yes, they sat with their friend in silence for seven days, feeling his pain. But then they undid all the good they had accomplished by savaging him with long, judgmental speeches.

Regrettably, Job's friends spouted religious clichés, lectured grandly on theology, then with worldly wisdom tried to explain what had happened to their devastated friend. Mostly, they pointed blame—not at the attacker, Satan, but at the victim, Job. They brought out all their lofty, spiritual-sounding ammunition and aimed it squarely at their hurting friend.

"Job, your suffering is your own fault; it has to be. You must have committed some unforgivable sin. You brought this evil on yourself." One after another after another, their accusations flew, leaving Job reeling.

Can you relate? At your lowest point, in the midst of your most painful trials, have people said such hurtful things to you? Have they spoken empty, comfortless words or given you meaningless, useless advice? Have they poured salt in your wounds? Criticized, judged, or even condemned you?

I know I can relate.

I knew very little about clinical depression before I ended up in the hospital with that diagnosis. I also knew nothing of the stigma that exists within the church regarding any kind of mental illness. I quickly learned a lot about both.

I could hardly believe the onslaught of hate-filled phone calls and letters I received from people I had counted as friends. It seemed they felt obligated to let me know exactly how angry and disappointed they felt with me. It had taken me far too long to admit that I needed help, but when I tried to get some, I promptly got condemned for it. People I had expected to lovingly support me instead declared:

"There must be sin in your life."

"You don't have enough faith!"

"You are a disgrace to the ministry."

"Christians should not need medication."

Someone I had known and loved for more than twenty years called me and said, "We are no longer friends. I want nothing more to do with you." I tried repeatedly to help this friend understand that I had not deliberately chosen to become mentally ill, to become completely overwhelmed by depression and despair. Whatever the reason for my condition, I needed him now more than ever.

But he had simply closed the door. He either couldn't or wouldn't hear me.

I wept many bitter tears over these assaults. Some critics simply didn't understand the nature of clinical depression and made their cruel comments in ignorance. Others apparently had seen me as a role model and couldn't bear to see me any other way—certainly not as a weak, frail, imperfect human being.

In no time at all I discovered that I had more enemies than just Satan. People with whom I had worked side by side in ministry actually seemed to celebrate my demise. I can still remember the night when a friend called to tell me some of the cruel things that were being said. I remember exactly where I was standing. I remember because I fell to my knees on the floor and wept. I honestly felt as if I were going to die. I could do nothing. I was broken, empty, and beyond exhausted. I had no strength left even to try to defend myself.

When betrayal comes from the hand of someone you trusted—or worse, from someone you loved—it pierces right to the core of your being. When I found myself in this unbearable and lonely place, it became clear to me that I had two choices:

1. I could submit myself to the Refiner's fire, believing that God is in control no matter how things appear; or
2. I could allow myself to get tossed around in the tormentor's cauldron—churned up like the sea, trying to put fires out, defending myself.

I had to ask myself a foundational question, just as you do when the words or actions of a friend wound you: is God in control? No matter who wields the sword: is God still sovereign?

Struggling with that question has been one of the most profoundly life-changing battles of my life. Everything within me screamed out, "But, Lord, it's not fair! I don't deserve this! They don't understand!" Having wrestled with God until I had no breath left, I came to understand something profound as the dust of my self-defense settled.

Fair does not live here, but Jesus does.

Not only that, but God is good and He can be trusted 100 percent of the time.

When we can give an absolute "yes!" to that question—the question of God's ultimate control and sovereignty—then we can submit ourselves to Him in anything. When we are set free from the need to be seen as right, then we can allow ourselves to bury our faces in the mane of the Lion of Judah—and there be loved.

Oh, for more expressions of compassionate, spectator grace! Oh, that we would choose to love and support—even in silence—rather than give free rein to our own misgivings and criticisms.

Our View of God and Others

Second, suffering tends to change how we see both God and others. To be frank, I don't always understand what God is thinking—what He is doing or not doing, and why. My tiny brain trying to understand His mind is like wiring a lightning bolt to a tiny flashlight bulb. But I have learned that suffering and pain peel back the layers of our faith and present us a life-changing choice: Will we become bitter, blaming God and others for our pain, venting our hurt and anger and frustration on those we consider responsible? Will we wallow in self-pity? Will we run and hide? Will we resist?

Or . . .

Will we choose to see God's hand in the midst of our pain and suffering? Will we embrace His will for us? Will we declare our trust in Him and fall at His feet in worship? Will we bring the broken pieces of our lives to Him and allow Him to use them to create something beautiful, something that brings Him glory?

Further, will we choose to use our pain and brokenness to help others who also travel this fearsome road? Will we choose to encourage them, instruct them, listen to them, support them, and gently point them to Jesus, even if they think He has abandoned them? And what will we choose to do with 2 Corinthians 1:3–7, which has volumes to say to those of us who belong to this fellowship of the broken?

> Praise be to the God and Father of our Lord Jesus Christ, the Father of compassion and the God of all comfort, who comforts us in all our troubles, so that we can comfort those in any trouble with the comfort we ourselves have received from God. For just as the sufferings of Christ flow

over into our lives, so also through Christ our comfort overflows. If we are distressed, it is for your comfort and salvation; if we are comforted, it is for your comfort, which produces in you patient endurance of the same sufferings we suffer. And our hope for you is firm, because we know that just as you share in our sufferings, so also you share in our comfort.

All of this is *huge*! Are we helpless victims in this broken world, or are we precious children, entrusted with suffering at times, for reasons we do not understand, by our Father who dearly loves us and who never takes His eyes off us?

I have lived—set up camp—in the valley of suffering and pain, and I can tell you with everything in me that I thank God for that place!

"But, Sheila," you say, "that's crazy! How can you thank God for something that almost destroyed you?"

I have a simple answer: it set me free. It set me free from the fear of man, from the fear of what others might say about me or do to me, from the fear of being open and vulnerable and known.

I wouldn't change a single moment because that despair and hopelessness led me to a place where I found true, lasting hope. When I had no strength left and nowhere to turn, I learned one of the most life-changing lessons ever:

> My God is my rock. I can run to him for safety. He is my shield and my saving strength, my defender and my place of safety. (2 Samuel 22:3 NCV)

God is *your* Rock, *your* Shield, *your* Defender too. In your darkest moments you will find that He is there. He is with you. He is for you. Nothing can happen to you unless God allows it, and if He allows it, He promises the grace and strength to walk through it—even if it forces you to your knees.

I know that sounds hard.

But it should.

Because it is.

For too long we have imbibed a watered-down, filtered version of the Christian faith—a faith that's all about us. A faith that claims life will always work out well. A faith that promises picture-perfect, happy families, healthy bank accounts, and good reports from our annual physicals.

But this is not the normal Christian life as described in the Word of God!

Jesus said to His disciples, His dearest friends on this earth, that the world would hate them because of Him. He told them to expect all kinds of trials and tribulations. "I told you these things," He said to them, "so that you can have peace in me. In this world you will have trouble, but be brave! I have defeated the world" (John 16:33 NCV).

The reality, of course, is that we live in a broken world. And we ourselves are broken, from the beginning. We can try to hide our brokenness or run from it. We can deny our brokenness or resist it. Or we can own our brokenness, embrace it, and bring it to God. If we will humble ourselves and bring our brokenness to Him, we will be amazed—even openmouthed *astounded*—at what He can do:

> God uses broken things. It takes broken soil to produce a crop, broken clouds to give rain, broken grain to give bread, broken bread to give strength. It is the broken alabaster box that gives forth perfume. It is Peter, weeping bitterly, who returns to greater power than ever.[26]

What Matters Most

Third, suffering changes what matters most to us. Before we suffer, we might value above all else a new home, a great job, a good name in the community, a robust bank account, a healthy body, or a happy family. After we have endured some period of suffering, it's not that those things lose all importance . . . they simply slide down the rubble-strewn mountain to their proper place, someplace well below the summit.

But again, we have to choose. Hardship and suffering by themselves will not teach us what to value preeminently. Hardship simply allows that choice to sink in and to stick like nothing else known to humankind.

I think here of the vast chasm that lay between the first two kings of ancient Israel, Saul and David. They had many things in common. The prophet Samuel anointed both men to serve as king. They both started out well. They both gained, at least for a time, the popular support of the people. They both led their armies to victories in battle. Both faced difficult, even terrifying situations. Both made choices that framed their respective reigns. But while one's choices doomed him, the other's choices elevated him.

It all came down to this: while David feared God, Saul feared everything else.

In Saul's story, from beginning to end, we see what happens when fear drives a person. After Samuel told Saul privately that God would make him king, you might have expected the young man to step up to the plate. But when the time came for him to be crowned, Saul hid himself "among the baggage," fearful of his calling (1 Samuel 10:22).

Fear also played a prominent role in the two incidents that together cost Saul his throne. In the second year of his reign, Saul and his newly formed army prepared to go into battle against the massive, well-trained army of the Philistines. Many of Saul's men ran away even before the fighting began. Samuel sent a message to Saul, telling him not to fear. Within seven days the prophet would arrive and offer sacrifices to the Lord, and then they would triumph.

Such simple instructions. It wasn't rocket science! "Don't do anything, Saul. Stand firm with the men you still have, and wait for me." But Saul, instead of throwing himself on the mercy of God, was doing calculations in his head. The longer he waited, the more men he would lose to desertion. In his worry and impatience, he thought he knew best. So although he was no priest, and Samuel had forbidden him to do so, he offered the sacrifices himself.

When Samuel finally arrived and saw what Saul had done, he declared that the king's rebellion and disobedience would cost him his kingdom. Saul made his apologies and had his excuses. But when you look beneath the verbiage, it becomes clear that he let his fear lead him into disobedience.

A little later God told Saul to destroy the Amalekites as punishment for their sins against Israel. But the disobedient king spared Agag, the ruler of the Amalekites, as well as the best of the sheep and oxen and fattened calves and lambs—along with anything else he thought looked good. He destroyed only what he considered "despised and worthless" (1 Samuel 15:9 ESV).

When Samuel again confronted Saul with his wickedness, the sullen king finally admitted what had driven him all along: "I was afraid of the people and so I gave in to them" (1 Samuel 15:24). Saul's attempt to cover his fear-driven sin with religious observance did not impress Samuel, who replied, "Does the LORD delight in burnt offerings and sacrifices as much as in obeying the voice of the LORD? To obey is better than sacrifice, and to heed is better than the fat of rams" (1 Samuel 15:22).

All his life, Saul feared everything but the Lord.

Eventually that fear cost him both his kingdom and his life.

What about you? What do you fear? Bankruptcy? Cancer? Paralysis? Loss of a spouse or a relationship? The uncovering of some secret sin? Humiliation? Scorn? What fears could drive you to make the same fatal choices that destroyed Saul?

Hardship, difficulty, and fear do not have to doom you to destruction. David also faced many hardships and difficulties, and yet the one fear that drove him—the fear of the Lord—made him into Israel's most beloved king.

Psalm 111:10 declares, "The fear of the LORD is the beginning of wisdom; all who follow his precepts have good understanding. To him belongs eternal praise."

To fear God, of course, doesn't mean to live in fear of Him. I know of some people who feel deathly afraid of God, frightened of what He might do to them, ask of them, require of them. They don't approach Him willingly, for fear that He might scorch them where they quiver. This is *not* what the Bible means by "the fear of the Lord."

And yet, at the same time, to fear God means more than merely to reverence Him, to hold Him in awe. Do you remember what happened shortly after the founding of the church? Two church members, the husband-and-wife team of Ananias and Sapphira, decided to lie to the Holy Spirit in the matter of giving an offering. God struck both of them dead for their deceit. The story ends with this postscript: "Great fear seized the whole church and all who heard about these events" (Acts 5:11).

To fear the Lord means you never forget who created the universe (with a word) and who describes Himself as "a consuming fire" (Hebrews 12:29). But it also means that you believe His promise that He will never leave or forsake those who put their trust in Him (see Deuteronomy 31:6, 8). And so, even in your suffering, you hear and take heart in the words of the prophet:

Who among you fears the LORD
and obeys the word of his servant?

Let him who walks in the dark,
who has no light,
trust in the name of the LORD
and rely on his God.

(ISAIAH 50:10)

David had that kind of fear of the Lord. His fear of God and trust in God empowered him to slay the giant Goliath (even as a boy), to take Jerusalem as his new capital (as a young king), and to lay the groundwork for the construction of the temple (as an old man). Even when he sinned terribly, as in his adultery with Bathsheba, the fear of the Lord finally won out over his lust and arrogance. As he would write after he had admitted and repented of his grave sin, "The sacrifices of God are a broken spirit; a broken and contrite heart, O God, you will not despise" (Psalm 51:17 ESV).

In sharp contrast to Saul, David owned and embraced his brokenness. And so he could write,

Purify me from my sins, and I will be clean; wash me, and I will be whiter than snow. Oh, give me back my joy again; you have broken me—now let me rejoice. (Psalm 51:7–8 NLT)

The Bible calls David a man after God's own heart,[27] not because he didn't sin—and sin in shocking, heartbreaking ways—but because he understood as deep as the marrow in his bones that he was a broken sinner and his only hope lay in God's forgiveness and restoration. Although he was far, far from perfect, all his life he remained passionate about loving the God who loved him.

Somehow David understood that brokenness presents no barrier between us and God, unless we make it one by stubbornly refusing to own it and accept it. If instead we can embrace our brokenness, we will find it becomes a path, rather than a barrier, that leads us to a deeper, richer, fuller relationship with God.

When deep suffering blasts into our lives and we choose to respond to it—even after a long struggle—with trust in God, we begin to see, clearer than we ever have, what truly matters in life. And then we can gladly join Asaph in one of the clearest expressions of true faith in the entire Bible:

Whom have I in heaven but you?
And earth has nothing I desire besides you.
My flesh and my heart may fail,
but God is the strength of my heart
and my portion forever.

(PSALM 73:25–26)

Nothing to Protect or Lose

How does brokenness change us? To sum it all up, perhaps I could say it like this: broken people have nothing to protect and nothing to lose.

They don't fear suffering, because they've chosen to use it to drive them into God's loving arms.

They don't fear men, because they know that who lives inside them is greater than whoever stands before them.

They don't fear death, because they know who and what awaits them on the other side.

Yes, brokenness changes us. I thank God that it has changed me! And one day in heaven, when I am no longer broken, I will continue to praise God's holy name for the breaking He oversaw in me on this side of heaven. And I will sing:

Give thanks to the LORD, for he is good;
his love endures forever.

(1 CHRONICLES 16:34)

Ten

CALLED TO SOMETHING BIGGER
Allow God to Use Your Pain for Heaven's Stunning Purposes

From five thousand feet, Manila reminded me of a disturbed ant colony, bustling, scurrying, almost frenetic with life.

I'd done a little homework before the trip and learned that this capital of the Philippines is the most densely populated city in the world, with almost 2 million souls packed into its twenty-three square miles. I was visiting there with a ministry called Operation Blessing, to distribute food, blankets, and basic medical supplies to many of the poorest of the poor.

Part of our itinerary included a visit to the city garbage dump. We wouldn't be there to throw anything away, but rather to help reclaim precious human lives from the desperate edge of poverty. Our actual task would be distributing blankets to the thirty thousand people who scrape out a living by sorting through great mounts of trash hauled in every day.

It's just a little difficult to comprehend this sort of life. These people—men, women, and children—get up before dawn with headlamps and baskets, waiting for the first truck to arrive at around 4:00 a.m. During the next seventeen hours, more than 430 trucks will dump a thousand tons of trash, which the people will gather in baskets and sort through to see what they can salvage and sell.

The next morning our team got up early too. We climbed into our jeeps before dawn and covered ourselves with high-octane bug spray. "Wear long socks and boots and long-sleeve T-shirts," they told us. At first that seemed crazy, as it gets sweleringly hot the minute the sun begins to rise. But I soon saw the wisdom of this unofficial dress code. Pictures can prepare you—a little—for the sight, but *nothing* prepares you for the smell and the noise that rise from a literal mountain of trash, or for the flies and mosquitoes that hover in clouds (explaining why I needed a long-sleeve shirt and socks).

Our drivers found a place to pull over and let us out as the Operation Blessing supply truck pulled in. I felt something brush against my leg, and expecting to find a dog, I bent down for a closer look. But no dog gazed back up at me. Instead, a hungry vulture brushed past me. A host of these scavengers swarmed the area where we stood. Having seen a *National Geographic* special that showed the malevolence of these creatures, I felt terrified . . . initially. Then I realized they had little interest in us. The vultures were lining up to pick through the trash, just like everyone else.

A Filipino staff member from Operation Blessing made an announcement over a bullhorn that we had come that day to give out blankets and water. He asked the people to line up so that we could begin distribution. Sitting in the back of a flatbed truck with blankets in hand, I expected a stampede—but none came. What I saw that day amazed me. These desperately poor people lined up in a very orderly fashion, and then those at the front of the line began to hand blankets back to the elderly and the disabled. Only when those who could not physically stand in line had been served did any of the others take anything for themselves.

We also passed out small New Testaments in the Filipino language, which the people received like bars of gold.

A local pastor helping us that day saw big tears rolling down my cheeks. "Are you okay?" he asked.

"Even though this is such a wasteland," I said, "I feel God's presence so profoundly here."

"Yes." He nodded. "God is very close to the poor and the destitute."

I will never forget those faces, big smiles barely disguising rotten teeth. Warm handshakes. Grateful hearts.

Back in the comfort of my hotel room that night, I found myself overwhelmed with emotion. I wept as I realized that darkness had now fallen at that dump, too, and those people continued to do all they could to provide for themselves and their families. I had prayed for God's protection with every blanket I passed out, but what we had brought seemed so little in the face of such enormous need. I wept to think that this was the only life these children had ever known or probably ever would know, and how hard their mothers and fathers worked to make no more than two dollars a day.

I wept, too, as it seemed to me that on that filthy mountain of trash, God had given me a glimpse of what it could look like to be the body of Christ—the strong serving the weak, the young helping the old, everyone taken care of, no one left behind. And all done in a spirit of gratitude. For me, the fragrance of love covered the stench even of a mountain of trash.

The day moved me more than I can describe.

It was a terrible day in my life.

It was also a great day in my life.

A Divine Perspective on "Great"

Broken people often think "the end" has come for them. The end of joy. The end of significance. The end of hope. They seldom realize that, from God's point of view, brokenness actually leads to a different "end" altogether: the death of self-centeredness, pride, and unconcern.

In His earthly ministry, Jesus labeled only two people as having "great faith." As it turns out, both of these individuals reached out to Him on behalf of someone else.

Not only that, but both of these individuals approached Him as outsiders, cast-offs, Gentile riffraff.

Not only that, but both sought Him out in the grip of great pain and anguish.

Not only that, but both presented themselves as needy, broken people.

And He called their faith "great."

It's interesting, isn't it? We never read of Jesus calling the faith of Peter "great"—even though he was only the second man in history to walk on water! As far as we know, Jesus never gave that commendation to John, James, or any of the other disciples. Usually when He called attention to their faith at all, He was calling attention to how *little* of it they displayed. Not once did He refer to the faith of the religious leaders or Jewish scholars as "great." He never said even His own mother had "great" faith.

But when two Gentile outsiders approached Him to ask for mercy on behalf of their broken loved ones, He declared that in them He had found "great" faith. And here we are reading about that faith over two thousand years later.

One instance occurred when a Roman centurion (I mentioned him briefly in chapter 4 as one who amazed Jesus with his faith), a leader of the hated foreigners who had conquered and occupied Israel, asked Jesus to heal a beloved servant who lay at home, paralyzed and suffering terribly. Jesus agreed to visit the centurion's home—but the soldier stopped Him.

"Lord," the man said, "I do not deserve to have you come under my roof. But just say the word, and my servant will be healed. For I myself am a man under authority, with soldiers under me. I tell this one, 'Go,' and he goes; and that one, 'Come,' and he comes. I say to my servant, 'Do this,' and he does it" (Matthew 8:8–9).

Not often does someone "astonish" the Lord, but that is exactly what this centurion did. *The Message* describes Jesus as "taken aback" in that moment (v. 10). Matthew tells us that Jesus turned to those with Him and said, "I tell you the truth, I have not found anyone in Israel with such great faith" (v. 10). And at "that very hour" the man's servant was healed (v. 13).

The second instance of "great faith" seems even more astonishing to me. This time, the person singled out for the designation was a distraught Canaanite woman from the pagan area of Tyre and Sidon. She approached Jesus to ask Him to free her daughter from the terrifying darkness of demon possession.

And at first, Jesus ignored her.

When she cried out, "Lord, Son of David, have mercy on me! My daughter is suffering terribly from demon-possession," Matthew says, "Jesus did not answer a word" (15:22–23).

This woman, however, refused to take silence for an answer! Love impelled her to keep seeking, keep knocking, and keep asking. She kept following the Lord and His group and crying out for mercy, so much so that His disciples finally asked Jesus to take stronger measures and send her away. So He turned to the woman and said, "I was sent only to the lost sheep of Israel"—a pointed reference to her non-Jewish status (v. 24).

But even this apparent rebuff didn't dissuade her.

She came right up to Jesus, knelt before Him, and humbly said, "Lord, help me!" (v. 25). Even then she didn't get a "yes"! What she got seems more like a slap in the face: "It is not right to take the children's bread and toss it to their dogs" (v. 26).

How would you have responded if you had come to Jesus for help and received such a cold answer? But it did not deter this woman, this anguishing mother-on-a-mission. "Yes, Lord," she replied, "but even the dogs eat the crumbs that fall from their masters' table" (v. 27).

This broken woman didn't care a fig for what anyone thought of her. The glares, frowns, and apparent rejection rolled right off her back. She embraced her brokenness in full—a woman in a male-dominated culture, a Canaanite in a Jewish society, a foreigner in a region not her own, a mother of a child inhabited by a filthy evil spirit—and her faith shone through *on behalf of someone else*.

Jesus looked at her and said, "Woman, you have great [Greek, *megale*] faith! Your request is granted" (v. 28). And once again, Jesus healed at a distance. Somewhere, perhaps miles away, a little girl instantly felt something slip away from her, as a peace like she'd never experienced settled in the deep places of her heart.

How I love stories like these! I am reminded once again how God delights in men and women reaching outside of themselves to do "great" things for others. He calls broken people not only to place their faith in Him, despite the darkness, but also to dare to reach beyond themselves and, through faith, bring the healing, loving touch of Christ to other hurting men and women.

This last account in particular also reminds me that reaching out to the living God in faith may not always be easy. We may have to battle through periods of unexplained silence. We may have to persevere in the face of apparent divine rebuffs. We may have to reach deep within to access the faith, already placed there by God Himself, that eventually wins the day.

God calls us—the broken, the hurting, the stumbling, the weak, the disadvantaged, and yes, even the foolish—to something bigger than our own comfort. He calls us to be the church for others.

A Time for Growing Up

To be the church for others, we need to have a faith that is deeply our own, a faith that stands apart from our upbringing. In his book *Changes That Heal*, Dr. Henry Cloud wrote, "When people begin to reason as adults, and not as black-and-white-thinking children, mystery and ambiguity become more acceptable, and love becomes more important."[28]

I watched this happen with our fifteen-year-old son recently. Christian has been a very compassionate boy since early childhood. At five years of age he asked me to pray with him, as he wanted to begin a relationship with Christ for himself. It has been beautiful to watch as his faith has matured over the last few years, particularly as it relates to becoming the heart and hands of Jesus to those around him. This year he moved into high school and has made some new friends.

One day as Christian, Barry, and I were driving home from church, Barry told Christian that he felt he should keep his distance from one boy who seemed troubled and was acting out at school. Christian agreed that the boy faced some tough times as his mom and dad tussled through a messy divorce. "I just think you might want to keep a distance from him for a while," said Barry, ever the protective dad.

Christian's answer moved me deeply.

"Dad," he replied, "I mean no disrespect, but I believe that I'm *meant* to be his friend. If I just walk away, how do I square that with God?"

Wow.

That is having a faith that is yours, a faith both real and deep. Growing in Christ means letting go of our need to understand or control everything, and letting go of our need for approval. The closer we approach the heart of Christ, the less our faith becomes about *us*, about what makes *us* feel good, and the more it becomes about others.

We will never become the church for others without first becoming mature in Christ. Mature believers become "like Christ." Even the name Christian means "little Christs."

And how do we become like Christ?

You may not like the biblical answer.

From all that I see in Scripture, *suffering* appears to have quite a bit to do with it. But then, why should that surprise us? We are told, after all, that in "bringing many sons to glory, it was fitting that God, for whom and through whom everything exists, should make the author of their salvation perfect through suffering" (Hebrews 2:10). Even Christ had to suffer in order to be made "perfect"!

Yes, but what does that really mean, anyway?

The word translated "perfect" in this passage plays such an important role in the book of Hebrews that the author uses it nine times. One commentator wrote that although the text has no *im*perfection in mind in regard to Jesus, "there is a perfection that results from actually having suffered and that this is different from the perfection of being ready to suffer. The bud may be perfect, but there is a difference between its perfection and that of the flower."[29]

So if Jesus Himself had to suffer to become "perfect" as our Savior, then how can we imagine that we wouldn't have to suffer, if our goal is to become like Him?

Can you imagine the apostle Paul nodding his head at this thought? While imprisoned in a Roman jail, he penned these words: "I want to know Christ and the power of his resurrection and the fellowship of sharing in his sufferings, becoming like him in his death" (Philippians 3:10).

James clearly had it in mind too: "Consider it pure joy, my brothers, whenever you face trials of many kinds, because you know that the testing of your faith develops perseverance. Perseverance must finish its work so that you may be mature and complete, not lacking anything" (James 1:2–4). Like it or not, embrace it or not, maturity comes, at least in part, through a godly response to suffering.

The suffering that helps us become like Christ also enables us and motivates us to become better and more willing servants. It's so true! And serving in turn plays a role in helping us become mature. Paul tells us that God gave various leaders to the church "to prepare God's people for works of service." For what reason? Service not only builds up the church, encourages unity, and helps us know Christ, but also equips us to "become mature," that we might attain "to the whole measure of the fullness of Christ" (Ephesians 4:11–13).

God uses both suffering and service to enable us to attain the whole measure of the fullness of Christ. But I think a third *S* also has an important part to play.

Scripture.

We will mature in Christ through suffering and service only when the living Word of God entwines through our experiences and our minds become more like the mind of Christ. While listening to good sermons can be incredibly helpful, and reading solid Christian books or tuning in to Bible-based radio broadcasts can encourage us in the process, nothing helps more than reading and studying God's Word for ourselves while asking the Holy Spirit to teach us.

And it's here, I think, where many of us slip a bit.

Dig for Yourself

When you grow up on the west coast of Scotland, it seems like you see sheep everywhere. In fact, if you land at Glasgow airport and drive the thirty miles southwest to my hometown of Ayr, you'll pass field after field after field of large, white woolly sheep.

I've often heard American tourists comment on how white the sheep look. Do you know why our sheep always look so white? It's simple: it's always raining! Any dirt or mud they get into quickly gets washed away.

In the winter of 2010, however, everything changed. The unusually harsh winter that year in Great Britain introduced sheep to a new reality—one that they had lost the instincts to cope with. I read about it in a British newspaper in an article titled "Snow Stories: Sheep Have Forgotten How to Cope with Snow."[30]

Twenty-five years of milder winters meant that the flocks had lost practice in finding shelters on hilltops—and shepherds had lost the habit of providing them. The article quoted Malcolm Corbett, who farms in the Northumberland National Park. Corbett explained that in the past, during fierce winters, shepherds gathered their flocks in "spells"—open, circular shelters—where they could find fodder left there for them. "The young ewes learn from the older ones to come in to the shelters during the bad weather, but that's not something they have had to do recently."

Apparently, even without man-made shelters, sheep can survive for long periods of time if they burrow down through a snowdrift and reach a food source. Corbett continued, "Animals evolve and so do their practices which maintain and sustain them in their environment, and this sheltering under the snow is something they have not required."

So in the winter of 2010, when four feet of snow lay on the fells, many sheep died. They didn't know that if they used their hooves, designed for digging, they could have dug deep and found what they needed to survive all winter long.

I couldn't help but see myself and many in the body of Christ in this story. We've become so accustomed to being hand-fed the Word of God, we've forgotten how to dig down even a little bit and forage for ourselves. Then life gets hard and winds blow and snow falls on our hearts—and we find we don't remember how to dig deep into God's Word to feed ourselves. So we begin to starve, even though all we need lies right there, waiting for us.

In a devotion he called "Prayerfully Ransack the Bible," John Piper insists that in "order to understand the Word of God, and delight in the God of the Word, and to be changed from the inside out, we must pray, 'Open my eyes that I may see wonderful things in your Law' (Psalm 119:18)."[31] But we must never set prayer and Bible study against each other, as if we had to choose between the two.

Piper gives four suggestions on how to dig into the Word.

First, *pray and read*. In Ephesians 3:3–4 Paul wrote, "By revelation there was made known to me the mystery, as I wrote before in brief. By referring to this, *when you read* you can understand my insight into the mystery of Christ" (NASB, emphasis added). Piper notes, "When you *read*! God willed that the greatest mysteries of life be revealed through reading . . . praying cannot replace reading. Praying may turn reading into seeing. But if we don't read we will not see. The Holy Spirit is sent to glorify Jesus, and the glory of Jesus is portrayed in the Word. So read."

Second, *pray and study*. We cannot accurately handle the Word of truth without spending time with it, meditating on it, studying it (see 2 Timothy 2:15). If we want to receive the most possible from God's Word—if we want to get at the food we need when the snow piles up in drifts—then we must work at the Word.

Third, *pray and ransack*. Piper suggests we approach the Bible "like a miser in the gold rush, or a fiancée who has lost her engagement ring somewhere in the house. She ransacks the house. That is the way we seek for God in the Bible." Proverbs 2:3–5 tells us, "If you cry for discernment, lift your voice for understanding; if you seek her as silver, and search for her as for hidden treasures; then you will discern the fear of the LORD and discover the knowledge of God" (NASB).

Do we truly believe the Bible contains hidden treasures? If so, we must act like it. And we should remember that God promises to give to those who seek Him with all their hearts (see Jeremiah 29:13).

Fourth, *pray and think*. Piper's translation of 2 Timothy 2:7 reads, "Think over what I say, for the Lord will give you understanding in everything." Although God "gives" us understanding, He normally does not do so without us first doing the hard work of thinking. "God has ordained that the *eye-opening work of his Spirit* always be combined with the *mind-informing work of his Word*," Piper wrote. "His aim is that we see the glory of God and that we reflect the glory of God. And so he opens our eyes when we are look-ing at the glory of God in the Word."

If food lies beneath the hooves of sheep in winter, how much more does treasure lie at our fingertips in the Word of God! But to benefit from it we must read it, ponder it, study it, pray over it. Only then will we receive the nourishment to keep us alive when the frigid winds howl and the ice covers our paths like a sheet. Amy Carmichael once wrote,

> Before the winds that blow do cease,
> Teach me to dwell within Thy calm;
> Before the pain has passed in peace,
> Give me, my God, to sing a psalm.
> Let me not lose the chance to prove
> The fullness of enabling love.
> O, Love of God, do this for me:
> Maintain a constant victory.[33]

Through the Roof

The creative young men described in Mark 2 went to remarkable lengths to help their ailing friend. They determined to bring him to Jesus, whatever the cost, so that he might get healed.

When they saw the large crowd around Jesus, they could have given up and said, "We'll try another time, another place, another day." Wouldn't you have done that? I think I might have. How could they get a poor man, who couldn't walk or even crawl, through a mob like that?

But in their love for him, they found a way.

As love usually does.

The typical Galilean home had a flat roof with an outside stairway or ladder leading to it. The roof, made of mud and reeds and branches, would get a remodeling job every fall before the onset of the winter rains.

I have no idea how those men managed to carry their paralyzed friend on his pallet up the ladder, but they did. Setting their friend down on the roof (can you imagine how intensely this disabled man must have been praying in that moment?) they began to dig. Imagine that you had been sitting inside that day, listening to Jesus, when bits of mud and broken branches suddenly started falling on your head! The friends must have taken out quite a bit of the roof, because they managed to lower the man on his mat right into the house.

There was nothing wrong with their aim either. They set their friend down right in front of Jesus.

I find it so compelling to see how Christ responded. He showed no anger—or even a flash of annoyance—because these men had interrupted His teaching. (Scripture doesn't tell us how Peter's *wife* felt about having part of her roof removed in the middle of a sermon.) We read instead that He "saw their faith." Others might have seen the mess or the inconvenience or the presumption.

But not Jesus.

Jesus saw their faith . . . and rewarded it. Their friend went home that day physically and spiritually whole.

Of course, many in those days needed healing—the blind, the lame, the injured, the maimed, the possessed, and the paralyzed. They all lined the streets, begging for help. What set this man apart (and put him in the Word of God for all eternity!) was that he had four friends who simply wouldn't give up on him.

I can imagine them that morning, looking into their paralyzed friend's eyes. "Don't worry," they may have told him. "One way or another, we're going to bring you to Jesus. You'll see!"

They epitomized the teaching of Christ: "A new commandment I give to you, that you love one another: just as I have loved you, you also are to love one another. By this all people will know that you are my disciples, if you have love for one another" (John 13:34–35 ESV). They had accepted God's call to something bigger, to be the church for others.

Have you accepted this call? Have I?

As I travel around the world, I see so many desperately lonely people within the church who long for the kind of friends the paralyzed man had—friends who simply refuse to give up on them. Friends who will carry them, if they can, or drag them, if necessary, to the throne of mercy. Let's not allow our self-focused, self-absorbed culture, or our overcrowded, stressed-out lives to rob us of the simple joy of caring for one another.

Despite our own pain, let's be the church for others.

Despite our own troubles, let's answer the call to something bigger.

Being broken changes the way we see each other. Those who understand that we all limp make better traveling companions.

And then let's watch in wonder as God does what only God can do.

ONLY THE WOUNDED CAN SERVE

What If Your Wounds Make You Fit for His Service?

A few years ago I picked up a copy of *The Collected Short Plays of Thornton Wilder*, volume 2 in a bookstore in Seattle, Washington.

I didn't know much of Wilder's work other than the play *Our Town*, but as I looked at the table of contents, one section in particular caught my attention.

The Angel That Troubled the Waters and Other Plays,

 Three-Minute Plays for Three Persons

I assumed Wilder had based his title play on the story found in John 5:1–9, about a lame man who had waited for years by a pool in Jerusalem, hoping for a touch of divine healing brought by an angelic messenger. So out of curiosity I purchased the book, wondering what the famed American playwright would make of this powerful story—in just three minutes!

I had no idea—although I'm pretty sure God did—what an impact it would have on my life.

The three characters in the play, loosely based on the story from John's gospel, include the Newcomer, the Mistaken Invalid, and the Angel. As the play opens, the Angel walks unseen among the broken, the blind, and the crippled. Only the moans of those in pain interrupt the silence. One of the sick, the Mistaken Invalid, suddenly wakes from a nightmare. Thinking that the Angel already has stirred the waters, he propels himself into the pool, only to realize his mistake and drag himself out of the water, disappointed yet again.

The Mistaken Invalid turns and sees the Newcomer standing beside him. He recognizes the man as his children's doctor and, seeing nothing wrong with him, snaps, "Go back to your work and leave these miracles to us who need them."

The Newcomer ignores the Invalid and continues to pray under his breath, pleading with God to heal him. Suddenly, the Angel makes himself visible to the Newcomer and asks him to step away from the water. The Newcomer begs for mercy, for though he appears whole on the outside, surely the Angel can see how badly battered and broken he is inside. The Angel acknowledges the Newcomer's brokenness, but tells him that the healing is not for him.

To this point in the play, I felt captivated by the writing and intrigued by the dialogue. But the next lines pierced my heart:

> The very angels themselves cannot persuade the wretched and blundering children on earth as can one human being broken on the wheels of living. In love's service only the wounded soldiers can serve. Draw back.[33]

"In love's service only the wounded soldiers can serve." What a powerful statement!

What if brokenness is a divine gift, a mystery we can fully understand and truly appreciate only in eternity?

What if our deepest wounds are the very places through which God's mercy flows to others?

What if instead of trying to fix ourselves, we present ourselves—broken and flawed though we are—to be used as He sees fit, for His glory and our good?

As Wilder's play draws to a close, the Mistaken Invalid sees the Angel trouble the water and makes it first into the pool. When he emerges whole and healed, he begs the Newcomer to come with him to his home: "My son is lost in dark thoughts, I . . . I do not understand him and only you have ever lifted his mood."[34]

What if the brokenness we ask God to fix is in fact a gift? What if the wounds we beg God to heal, the burdens we plead with Him to remove, are the very things that make us fit for His service?

Can our brokenness be a blessing?

Broken to Serve

I don't know what spiritual commitments Thornton Wilder may have made in his lifetime, but by his death in 1975, he had won three Pulitzer Prizes and one

National Book Award, among other honors—and several of his works focus on some aspect of spirituality. While his father served as a U.S. consul general in China, Wilder studied at a China Inland Mission school. Later in life he met the existentialist Jean-Paul Sartre and even translated some of the Frenchman's work into English; but Wilder rejected Sartre's atheism.

While most critics regard *The Angel That Troubled the Waters* as Wilder's first successful dramatic work (1928), a few years later (1935) he would write *Heaven's My Destination*, a Depression-era story about an itinerant salesman of religious books. And his Pulitzer Prize—winning novel *The Bridge of San Luis Rey* (1927) explores the "problem of evil" and why bad things happen to apparently innocent people. Wilder clearly knew at least some aspects of Scripture, and many of its major themes seem to have prompted him to put pen to paper.

I can't get past that idea whenever I ponder *The Angel That Troubled the Waters*. You don't write a play like that without knowing the Bible, and you don't write a line such as "In love's service only the wounded soldiers can serve" unless you know something of being broken yourself. Wilder served in both World War I and World War II, and no doubt saw a lot of broken people in those two terrible conflicts.

Did he also recognize the power of brokenness in most of the Bible's biggest heroes?

If you were to name the two individuals in Scripture, outside of the Lord Himself, who in their lifetimes provided the most profound, life-changing service to others, who would you pick?

My own choices probably surprise no one. For the Old Testament I'd pick Moses and for the New Testament I'd pick Paul. No offense to Abraham or David, Peter or John, but I think Moses and Paul "out-served" everyone else in their respective Testaments.

And both were badly broken.

Although Moses grew up in the privileged royal court of Egypt, he never got to know his biological parents as Mom and Dad. They had to give him up as a baby to save his life, and such a forced separation nearly always leaves scars. Did it make him angry? Maybe. Clearly, he had a temper; at forty years of age he had to flee Egypt after in anger he killed an Egyptian whom he saw mistreating some Hebrew slaves. A conspicuous childhood stutter also followed him into adulthood, an embarrassing disability that he thought disqualified him from serving God. Moses had some serious self-image problems! [35]

And yet God took this orphaned, stuttering, murdering refugee and turned him into Israel's lawgiver, a man who 3,500 years later still elicits admiration and even awe from Jews and Christians alike. Through Moses, God gave us five books of the Old Testament and one psalm (90).

In love's service, Moses certainly qualifies as a wounded soldier.

A millennium and a half after Moses' death, a man who labeled himself a "Hebrew of Hebrews" (Philippians 3:5) also joined the ranks of God's suffering servants. Paul, too, became a superior divine servant only after he had suffered tremendously.

Unlike Moses, however, Paul grew up with both his parents, who apparently had either the connections or the money to confer Roman citizenship upon their son at his birth. They sent him to the finest schools, and eventually he studied under Gamaliel, the top Jewish scholar of his day. Paul's zeal for God eventually led him to persecute the early Christians, imprisoning or killing them in a furious effort to stamp out the young church.

But a funny thing happened to Paul on his way to further mayhem.

He met the very last person he ever expected to meet.

The risen Lord Jesus stopped him in his tracks, used a blinding shaft of light to knock him off his high horse, and then brought this violent, blaspheming man to saving faith in Christ.

How would you like to have been Ananias, the terrified Christian whom God tapped to point Paul to faith? Ananias wanted no part of *that* job! It would have been like receiving a divine summons to take a gospel tract to Hitler in his Berlin bunker.

The Lord, however, let Ananias know that He was quite serious about this. And then He said a very interesting thing about Paul: "I will show him how much he must suffer for my name" (Acts 9:16).

It's not that Paul would simply suffer for the name of Christ. The Lord told Ananias He intended to *show* Paul how much he would suffer, before the pain actually hit. And as we follow Paul's missionary career through the book of Acts, we see the Lord fulfilling His word. At one point, years later, Paul told some worried friends, "In every city the Holy Spirit warns me that prison and hardships are facing me" (Acts 20:23).

We get deeper insight into the scope of Paul's suffering for Christ in his own letters. In Galatians, for example, he wrote, "As you know, it was because of an illness that I first preached the gospel to you." In fact, it was illness so severe that he called it a "trial" for the Galatians. In other words, whatever Paul's affliction was it could have prompted these believers to treat him with contempt or scorn (4:13–14). In Philippians he recounted how his Christian witness landed him in jail and in chains (1:13), and in the city of Ephesus he remembered fighting "wild beasts" for the cause of Jesus (1 Corinthians 15:32). But we get the most graphic picture of his suffering and brokenness from the second letter he wrote to the Corinthian church. Listen to this amazing recital in the J. B. Phillips translation:

> I have worked harder than any of them. I have served more prison sentences! I have been beaten times without number. I have faced death again and again.
>
> I have been beaten the regulation thirty-nine stripes by the Jews five times.
>
> I have been beaten with rods three times. I have been stoned once. I have been shipwrecked three times. I have been twenty-four hours in the open sea.
>
> In my travels I have been in constant danger from rivers and floods, from bandits, from my own countrymen, and from pagans. I have faced danger in city streets, danger in the desert, danger on the high seas, danger among false Christians. I have known exhaustion, pain, long vigils, hunger and thirst, going without meals, cold and lack of clothing.
>
> Apart from all external trials I have the daily burden of responsibility for all the churches. . . .
>
> In Damascus, the town governor, acting by King Aretas' order had men out to arrest me. I escaped by climbing through a window and being let down the wall in a basket. That's the sort of dignified exit I can boast about. (2 Corinthians 11:23–28, 32–33)

Paul was no masochist. He didn't *like* suffering any more than we do. So he told us that he made a concerted effort in prayer to ask God to remove from him some unnamed trouble, which he called a "thorn in my flesh, a messenger of Satan"—something that constantly tormented him (2 Corinthians 12:7).

Paul prayed earnestly . . . and God said no.

As a result, the stricken apostle learned to accept his ongoing broken-ness as a gift from God, designed to help him serve wounded people more effectively.

By the end of his life (via the sharp edge of an executioner's sword), Paul had founded countless churches throughout the Mediterranean and penned no fewer than thirteen New Testament books. He served, and he served, and he served . . . all while desperately broken.

His life proves that in love's service, only the wounded can serve.

But I'm Too Broken!

Some of us have endured such heartbreak, suffered such tragedy, tolerated such unrelenting pain that we think, *I'm too broken to serve! I can hardly get up in the morning. I can hardly speak without weeping. How can you expect me to serve?*

Believe me, I'm not pushing you to do anything that might send you over the edge. I, too, have walked that narrow pathway next to the cliff; I, too, have felt the vertigo of those high and lonely places.

And yet . . .

An old Chinese fable tells of a woman who had only one child, a little boy. When her son died at an early age, a deep sorrow overwhelmed her and threatened to destroy her. One day, in utter torment, she visited a wise man to ask for help. The man told her, "Yes, I can help you. I have some magic that has the power to ease your sorrow. But you must do what I say. Go from house to house in your village and acquire one mustard seed from a family that has never felt the sting of deep sorrow."

As soon as the woman left the wise man, she returned home and started visiting one family after another. In her whole village, she found not one family that had managed to avoid sorrow, and so she did not obtain her magic mustard seed. But as her wounded and broken neighbors poured out their heartaches, tragedies, and losses, she listened . . . and the experience changed her life. Somehow, she began to minister to them. Eventually she began to realize that at least a portion of her sorrow grew less acute when she reached out to others in service. As she began to help others deal with their sorrow, her own spirits began to lift.

My friend, I'm not writing this chapter to coerce you into *anything*.

I have no desire to push you, shame you, or guilt-trip you into reaching out to the wounded around you. I have written this book to help you come to grips with your brokenness, so that you might again see the light of God pour into your darkened world. I wouldn't dream of burdening you with yet another "have to" that would only add to the heavy weight now pressing down on your shoulders. That's never been my intent, from page 1.

But I also know that burdens can be of more than one type. And I think it's important for us, the broken, to understand what sort of burdens confront us.

Too Much to Carry

One of the first verses I memorized as a young believer was Galatians 6:2: "Bear one another's burdens, and so fulfill the law of Christ" (ESV).

I don't know how to explain it, but I've always felt drawn to this call to community—to be there for each other. I loved the idea that we don't have to carry our heartaches by ourselves.

And it really sounds so simple, doesn't it? *Let's help each other carry our stuff because life is hard. It's what Jesus would do, right?* The trouble is that if you are tenderhearted or misunderstand the text, you might very well spend the rest of your life trying to help someone carry his load—without ever seeing that person grow any stronger. Instead, the individual you have devoted yourself to helping might become weaker and weaker, leaning more heavily on you every day.

Perhaps you are there now. You want do the right thing, but you feel increasingly drained day after day. Does Paul *really* call us to this?

But reading on to Galatians 6:4–5 (ESV), we come to this: "But let each one test his own work, and then his reason to boast will be in himself alone and not in his neighbor. For each will have to bear his own load."

What? Is this a contradiction? Why would the Bible say to "bear one another's burdens" and then turn around and say, "Each will have to bear his own load"?

In the original language, the word translated "burden" described a ship's full load—in other words, what any men or women would find too hard to carry by themselves. The word *load*, however, means a heavy thing carried by an individual, the amount of work to be done by one person. Do you see what a significant difference that makes?

It's the difference between carrying a grand piano on your back or strapping on a five-pound backpack.

At times in life we walk through things that simply prove too much for any one of us to bear alone—the death of a child, the end of a marriage, the loss of a home. In those times God calls us to carry one another's burdens, for who can bear a full ship's load alone? But each of us does receive a day's load to carry by ourselves. Christ calls us to look to Him for the strength to carry what He gives us every day. Even there, His promise lifts us up, for He won't ask us to do more than we can.

Remember these comforting words of Christ: "Come to me, all who labor and are heavy laden, and I will give you rest. Take my yoke upon you, and learn from me, for I am gentle and lowly in heart, and you will find rest for your souls. For my yoke is easy, and my burden is light" (Matthew 11:28–30 ESV). I love how Eugene Peterson presents it in *The Message*: "Are you tired? Worn out? Burned out on religion? Come to me. Get away with me and you'll recover your life. I'll show you how to take a real rest. Walk with me and work with me—watch how I do it. Learn the unforced rhythms of grace. I won't lay anything heavy or ill-fitting on you. Keep company with me and you'll learn to live freely and lightly."

I see such *freedom* in this fuller understanding of this text. Don't you?

God isn't calling us to step into someone's life and pick up the daily cross Jesus intends for him or her to carry as he or she follows Him. No, because that would even be damaging to that man or woman. How would he or she ever grow stronger in faith if we kept doing that *for* the person? Jesus doesn't ask us to be enablers or codependents. Not at all! Instead, the Lord calls each one of us to carry what He has given us. But in those times when brothers or sisters feel overwhelmed by a crushing weight that can't be borne alone, we step into their lives in the name of Jesus and help them until they can stand on their own again.

A Peculiar Grace

Even as I acknowledge that God calls each of us to carry our own load, it seems to me that in God's kingdom some are given what I call a peculiar grace, through brokenness, that marks them for life and draws others to them. I can think of a number of such people in my own life, a list of those who have suffered greatly and who, rather than turning in on themselves in their pain, became like a beacon in the night for others. While I don't for a moment intend to add my name to that list, I had an unusual encounter at one of the worst moments in my life that helped me see an aspect of grace I had not anticipated.

After my monthlong stay in the psychiatric hospital, I had no idea what I would do with the rest of my life. At thirty-six years of age, all I had known to that point was public ministry, whether as a singer or TV host. So far as I knew, those days had ended forever. I had heard as much from one staff member at the Christian Broadcasting Network who told me, "Once people know where you have been, no one will ever trust you again."

I assumed he was right.

I took his words as fact.

As a result, I decided to return to seminary, with no thought of preparing for ministry. After all, I'd let all that go. I went simply for my soul's sake, for personal enrichment. I moved from Virginia Beach on the East Coast to California on the West Coast, and there enrolled in Fuller Theological Seminary.

I had just started settling in when some friends asked if I'd like to attend a four-day intensive seminar on Christian living. I believe I told them I'd rather stick my hand in a blender. I felt worn-out and sad and had no desire to be with anyone other than my fellow students. But my friends persisted, telling me that they had been before and found it life changing.

"Life change"?

Hadn't I had enough of that for a century or two?

Again, I told my friends no. And again, my friends refused to take no for an answer. One friend said, "Okay, listen, I've *paid* for you to go. Just go for the first day. If you hate it, don't go back."

I finally agreed to go—but only because I knew they cared about me. One day of this thing would be enough and more than enough. After that, I'd make my excuses and leave.

I ended up, however, staying for the entire weekend.

About forty of us went through various exercises to show us who we really were and what we truly believed. I had mixed feelings about much of the weekend, since I'm not a fan of high emotion combined with low biblical content. Some of the exercises seemed designed to stir up past pain without the environment to lovingly deal with it. Even so, God used one particular moment to speak deeply into my heart.

Organizers gave each of us a Popsicle stick and then explained the rest of the exercise. We were to imagine ourselves on a sinking boat, but our life-boat lacked enough seats to save everyone. Each of us had to entrust our stick to the one person we believed would tell our loved ones how much they meant to us, the one person who would live on to make a difference in the world. I gave my stick to a guy who said his sole purpose in attending was to love his wife and daughters better. I had watched him own up to mistakes he'd made and cry bitter tears, but also commit to be a different man, with God's help.

I believed him.

Even the thought of "making a difference" felt overwhelming to me at that point, so although we were directed to stand in a circle, I knelt on the floor with my eyes closed. As music played, it felt as though I were watching a movie of all my years in public ministry, trying to get it right and to be strong—and now I sat in this place, profoundly broken and impossibly weak.

"Do you see what's happening?" a seminar facilitator whispered in my ear. I opened my eyes to see what he was talking about . . . and there at my feet I saw a pile of Popsicle sticks. It looked like everyone had given *me* his or her stick.

"I don't want this!" I said through tears. "I have nothing left to give."

"Everyone here seems to feel differently about that," he said.

I still have every one of those sticks. I keep them in a glass jar in my office. I don't keep them to remind myself that I was voted onto the boat. I keep them to remind myself that, rather than a curse, in Christ's wounded hands brokenness is a gift, an honor . . . a peculiar grace.

The Companionship of Brokenness

A few years ago I received a letter from a ministry leader asking if I would meet privately with his wife. He saw that I was to be in town to speak at a women's event and wrote, "A group of women from my church will attend, but my wife is not one of them. She is struggling with great sadness from her past that weighs her down." He told me that she really believed that if

anyone knew of her struggles, it would damage his reputation and hurt his ministry. He clearly did *not* believe that, but felt powerless to convince her.

I arranged for a private meeting room and said that if she would be willing to meet, I would gladly visit with her.

At first she wouldn't even make eye contact with me, so I said, "You don't have to tell me anything about your life. But I would love to tell you a little about mine."

I told her about the shame I had felt.

I told her that I believed I had failed God and everyone else.

I told her I had soaked the carpet with my tears, night after night after night.

I told her I believed that the darkness would never lift and that I had prayed to die.

And I told her about the hope I had found.

I told her that I still take medication, and every morning I take that little pill with a prayer of thanksgiving that God had made a way for those of us who suffer like this on such a broken planet. And I told her that in the darkest moment of my life, I discovered that God lives very close to the floor, very near to those who are broken.

For as long as I live, I will never forget the look in her eyes as she finally lifted her gaze from the floor to my face. It is no coincidence that God placed our tear ducts in our eyes! Pain should be seen. With tears pouring down her cheeks, she fell into my arms and we wept for a long time. The time for words had passed. We found a depth of understanding, of companionship, that went above and beyond anything either one of us could say. I prayed for her before she left and as she ran into her husband's arms. She was on the road to healing, perhaps not shedding her affliction but feeling God's acceptance in the midst of it.

It is a beautiful gift of grace to serve in our brokenness. Not everyone understands this. Not everyone is willing to be broken. But when you are broken in the hands of the Master, you would never, ever go back to living the illusion that you are, in your own strength, "whole."

THE SACRED ACHE

How God Transforms Your Hurts into Something Holy

Twenty-plus years ago, Jerry Sittser and his family were returning home in their minivan from a fun-filled day of learning about Native American culture and history.

Jerry remembers glancing up the highway and seeing a car in the distance, coming up on them fast, drifting across the center line. Approaching a curve, Jerry touched his brakes, pulling over as far as he could to get out of this crazy driver's way.

To no avail.

With an intoxicated driver behind the wheel, the car jumped lanes and, at eighty-five miles an hour, plowed into the Sittsers' vehicle head-on.

One instant later, Jerry's wife, Lynda; his four-year-old daughter, Diana Jane; and his mother, Grace, all lay dead.

"Three generations—gone in an instant!"

That's what Jerry wrote in a compelling and poignant book titled *A Grace Disguised: How the Soul Grows Through Loss*.[36]

Jerry's book has helped untold thousands of readers since its release in 1995, and an expanded edition nine years later has helped even more. But the author insists he didn't write his book "to help anyone get over or even through the experience of catastrophic loss."

Why would he say that? Because Jerry Sittser believes "that 'recovery' from such loss is an unrealistic and even harmful expectation, if by recovery we mean resuming the way we lived and felt prior to the loss." So why did he write the book? He did it "to show how it is possible to live in and be enlarged by loss, even as we continue to experience it. . . . My aim is not to provide quick and painless solutions but to point the way to a lifelong journey of growth."[37]

It sounds like Jerry has in mind what I call "the sacred ache."

A Supernatural Transformation

In a fallen world like this one, pain and suffering come to us all. Tragedy strikes; accidents happen; illness hits; loss intrudes; the unthinkable somehow becomes reality. Even for Christians. Even for obedient, filled-with-the-Spirit, faithful, on-fire followers of Jesus Christ.

Steve Brown puts it like this: "I have never understood how Christians who claim to follow the One who ended up hanging spread-eagle on the town garbage heap between two thieves could ever come up with the crazy ideas that life is easy, that we won't suffer, and that God's primary purpose in the world is to make us happy and to give us the good life."[38]

Amen, Steve. You and I both know that the ache of this world comes to us all.

But the *sacred* ache? That's a much different story.

Pain is just pain. But when we choose to take that pain and present it to God for His sovereign use, then that pain becomes *sacred*. Yes, we all have to deal with pain in the course of our lives—physical, emotional, and spiritual pain. But if we give God access to this pain, asking Him to turn it into something He can use . . . something happens. Something supernatural. In this new, potent, and divinely appointed role, it can remind us of a home we've never seen, even as it keeps us focused on our calling here on this troubled planet.

"Loss," says Jerry Sittser, "is like a terminal illness. There is nothing we can do to spare ourselves from such sickness, except perhaps put it off for a while. But there is another sickness that we can heal—the sickness of our souls. In matters of the soul, I do not want to treat symptoms but to heal the illness. If we face loss squarely and respond to it wisely, we will actually become healthier people, even as we draw closer to physical death. We will find our souls healed, as they can only be healed through suffering."[39]

Keep in mind that these words came from a man who lost his wife, his daughter, and his mother in one horrifying instant, through no fault of his own. In the pages of his book, he describes how the agony of his loss nearly consumed him. Depression overwhelmed him, and for a time he thought he would surely lose his mind. His once well-ordered life devolved into chaos.

He cried for forty days straight after the accident.

And then . . . his mourning turned into something too deep for tears. Truthfully, he would have welcomed tears as a respite from the relentless, soul-deep ache that gripped him from the moment he opened his eyes in the morning.

Yes, he would have liked to cry, but no tears came. He had all but dried up.

Over time, however, Jerry learned how to turn his pain over to God. That didn't make his grief disappear. It *still* hasn't disappeared, even two decades later.

Nevertheless, Jerry could write, "Pain and death do not have the final word; God does." And what does that final divine word say to a broken man such as Jerry? What "good" could it possibly create in such a broken life? Jerry wrote,

> I find myself thinking often about heaven. Life on earth is real and good. I once enjoyed it with the loved ones whom I lost, and I still enjoy it without them. But life here is not the end. Reality is more than we think it to be. There is another and greater reality that envelops this earthly one. Earth is not outside heaven, as the philosopher Peter Kreeft wrote; it is heaven's workshop, heaven's womb. My loved ones have entered that heaven and have joined those who died before them. They are in heaven now because they believed in Jesus, who suffered, died, and was raised for their sake. They live in the presence of God and in a reality I long to enter, but only in God's good time. . . . Heaven is our real home, where we have always longed to be.[40]

Longing is a key aspect of the sacred ache. Call it the bittersweet companion of hope. We long for what we do not yet have, remembering what we once had. Jerry Sittser admits that the accident that killed three precious members of his family still bewilders him. Although good came from it, he will never call the accident good. To him, it remains horrible, tragic, and evil. He doesn't believe the crash occurred in order that he might change for the better, rear three healthy children, or write a long-selling book.

No, to this day, he still wants his loved ones back.

He says he always will, regardless of any good their deaths might bring, either now or in the future.

"Yet the grief I feel is sweet as well as bitter," he wrote. "I still have a sorrowful soul; yet I wake up every morning joyful, eager for what the new day will bring. Never have I felt as much pain as I have in the last three years; yet never have I experienced as much pleasure in simply being alive and living an ordinary life. Never have I felt so broken; yet never have I been so whole. Never have I been so aware of my weakness and vulnerability; yet never have I been so content and felt so strong. Never has my soul been more dead; yet never has my soul been more alive."[41]

These battling words provide a memorable picture of the sacred ache. No wonder Jerry speaks of his soul being "stretched"! But above all, he says, he has become aware of the power of God's grace and of his need for it: "My soul has grown because it has been awakened to the goodness and love of God. God has been present in my life these past three years, even mysteriously in the accident. God will continue to be present to the end of my life and through all eternity. God is growing my soul, making it bigger, and filling it with himself. My life is being transformed. Though I have endured pain, I believe that the outcome is going to be wonderful."[42]

There you hear the essence of the sacred ache's power.

Yes, the pain lingers. It throbs sometimes like an old piece of shrapnel embedded in living bone. It ripples down across the days, months, years, and even decades. But whereas a mere ache crushes the soul into powder, even into nothingness, the sacred ache somehow enlarges the soul and makes it bigger to accommodate more of God.

And more of God, no matter what, is good.

How is this all possible? I don't know.

But I know it's true.

No Tear Forgotten

In the midst of our pain and grief—and especially at the front end—we may imagine God has abandoned us, forgotten us, dismissed us, or simply ignored us. We're not the first occupants of this broken planet to feel this way, nor will we be the last. Even a quick stroll through the Psalms reveals how often human thoughts wander down this shadowy pathway:

- "My soul is in anguish. How long, O Lord, how long?" (Psalm 6:3).
- "How long, O Lord? Will you forget me forever? How long will you hide your

face from me? How long must I wrestle with my thoughts and every day have sorrow in my heart? How long will my enemy triumph over me?" (Psalm 13:1–2).

- "How long, O LORD? Will you hide yourself forever? How long will your wrath burn like fire? Remember how fleeting is my life. For what futility you have created all men!" (Psalm 89:46–47).

- "Relent, O LORD! How long will it be? Have compassion on your servants. Satisfy us in the morning with your unfailing love, that we may sing for joy and be glad all our days. Make us glad for as many days as you have afflicted us, for as many years as we have seen trouble" (Psalm 90:13–15).

The prophet Habakkuk got in the act, too, crying out, "How long, O LORD, must I call for help, but you do not listen?" (1:2).

That's how we *feel*, and God seems to have no problem with our expressing it. So when you cry out to the Lord, asking Him your own version of "How long?" recognize that you're in good company.

But please don't leave it there. Don't allow your ache to remain merely an ache. Remember the truth, and allow that truth to seep into your troubled mind so that your ache might begin its transformation into something sacred. Remember what David whispered to God, after yet another near-death escape?

> *You keep track of all my sorrows.*
> *You have collected all my tears in your bottle.*
> *You have recorded each one in your book.*
>
> (PSALM 56:8 NLT)

Why would He do that? Why would God keep track of all our sorrows? Why would He collect all our tears in a bottle? Why does the Lord record each heartache, each grief, each sadness in some divine journal inscribed with heavenly ink?

It's because He has plans for those things.

It's because He wastes *nothing*.

He intends to fill our sorrows and tears with His expansive love. This was the glorious expectation of both the prophets and the apostles when each said of God:

He will swallow up death forever; and the Lord GOD will wipe away tears from all faces. (Isaiah 25:8 ESV)

He will wipe every tear from their eyes. There will be no more death or mourning or crying or pain, for the old order of things has passed away. (Revelation 21:4)

When we remember this—when we recall that God *does* in fact notice our pain, that He collects each tear in a bottle so that one day He might replace each teardrop with an ocean of divine love—our souls stop shrinking and begin to expand. The small world of our pain gives way to something boundless . . . beyond measure . . . beyond our reckoning.

God's incomprehensible love.

This is the biblical truth. This is the Christian's hope. And this is the sacred ache.

Beauty as Well as Hope

Did you know that this sacred ache can be beautiful as well as hopeful? That is why so many write of this unexpected gift. What I have discovered in my own life is that some of God's most profound gifts come in boxes that make our hands bleed as we open them—but then as we look inside the box, we find something we have been longing for all of our lives. Leigh McLeroy wrote about this phenomenon in her book *The Beautiful Ache: Finding the God Who Satisfies When Life Does Not*. What is this beautiful ache? Leigh wrote,

The beautiful ache is that fleeting pang that reminds us of home. Not the home we've always known—the home we've never seen. The ache pierces and pries open the heart but doesn't nearly satisfy it. It whets the appetite but doesn't begin to fill it. It unmasks beauty but not completely. It reeks of truth but stops just short of telling all.

Hardly a day goes by that I don't feel it. The trick is learning to allow the ache to take me where it wants to go, to tutor and tantalize my mostly numb senses with its laser-sharp aim. The challenge is to not kill it off before it fully arrives or dismiss it before it is ready to go.[43]

In fact, says Leigh, "the beautiful ache points us beyond. It is not meant to be ignored. So when it comes—and it will—why not move in closer and ask the ache what true and terrible secrets it knows and longs to tell? You won't regret it."[44]

Kari Lundberg knows all about the "true and terrible secrets" that such a beautiful, sacred ache has hidden away for us. I first made Kari's acquaintance probably thirty years ago, when I served with her husband, Ake Lundberg, during a Luis Palau evangelistic tour through several cities in the United Kingdom. While I sang and Ake snapped pictures, Kari fought her own spiritual battles, far from the glare of stage lights.

Dave and Jan Dravecky sketched out Kari's story in their book *Portraits in Courage*, a collection of deeply moving tales that describe ordinary people struggling heroically against breathtaking pain. Kari has suffered intensely for more than forty years with a wide range of ailments. "In the Western world," she says, "we feel offended at the fact that we suffer. We think, *God surely has an obligation to see to it that nothing nasty befalls me!* And our constant wail is, 'Why me?' In my own decades of intense pain and suffering, I have found that my only satisfaction is found in the words of Job 19:25 (NASB)—'And as for me, I know that my Redeemer lives.'"[45]

Kari had a difficult time from the very moment of her birth. She arrived in Oslo during the German occupation of Norway in World War II. Snow fell that night, along with the bombs of the Luftwaffe. Every night she and her family members went to bed with their clothes on, ready to scamper to the bomb shelter at a moment's notice. At age four she came down with tuberculosis, which she promptly gave to her mother. Doctors placed the two in different facilities for four long months, which Kari remembers as being far more difficult than fighting the disease. "Yet even at this young age," she said, "I had been introduced to the faith of my parents. I was taught that no matter our circumstances, Christ himself would sustain us. We may find ourselves in desperate circumstances, but God will provide the means by which we will ultimately be redeemed."[46]

After the war ended, Kari became active in the Salvation Army. She graduated early from college and soon got a call from a Norwegian-speaking church in Brooklyn, asking if she would come to minister. She left for the United States, where she met Ake; the two soon married and had a son, Sven. One day when Kari bent over the crib to pick up her baby, she let out bloodcurdling scream. During a subsequent five-hour surgery, doctors discovered she had a degenerative disc disease. For many weeks afterward she lay flat on her back in the hospital. One day she woke up with an excruciating headache, bringing yet another diagnosis, this time encephalitis and spinal meningitis. She slipped into a coma.

Doctors did not have good news for Ake: "Go home and prepare the funeral," they instructed him. On the fourth day of Kari's coma, students and staff of the seminary where both she and Ake attended held an all-night prayer vigil. They started at eleven in the evening and continued until eleven the following morning. Fifteen minutes after they ended their vigil, Kari sat up in bed and asked for breakfast; two days later she walked out of the hospital under her own power.

A miracle? Quite possibly. But even miracles may bow to the power of sacred aches.

When Ake got a job as a photographer with Billy Graham's *Decision* magazine, the Lundbergs moved to Minneapolis, Minnesota. A year later Kari had another back surgery, followed by three more, and then several other surgeries unrelated to her back. Some "callous Christians" (Kari's term) intensified her suffering by telling her, "You are suffering because you have too little faith," or "There must be hidden sin in your lives; otherwise you would be healed." Kari remembers, "The darkness of the night almost consumed me and I had nothing in my hands with which to fight back."[47] Still, she says, "I believed God is love, and although my faith wobbled, it did not fall down. God is the giver of all good gifts, and I knew He does not zap someone for lack of something better to do."[48]

Back in 1998, when Kari wrote her chapter for *Portraits*, she had endured eight back surgeries, seven other surgeries, and multiple kidney failures. She also suffered from arthritis, fibromyalgia, chronic fatigue syndrome, and decades of debilitating, chronic pain. Eventually she had a narcotics pump delivery system implanted in her body to help her deal with the pain.

Twice the Lundbergs have run out of insurance coverage. Yet Kari says that countless times she has been reminded that our Redeemer lives. And she quotes Job: "After my skin has been destroyed, yet in my flesh I will see God; I myself will see him with my own eyes—I, and not another" (Job 19:26–27).

A phone conversation with Kari in just the past few days updated me on her struggles. Since her 1998 article, she has undergone yet more surgeries, has developed a heart condition, and suffers from shingles. She reports, "Four years ago I broke my neck, and now I'm in a wheelchair most of the time. I know what suffering is. But my heart and soul are well. We need to learn to admit the suffering and being honest. But for me, it has brought me into a much deeper prayer life. And God has helped me develop a great sense of gratitude for what I do have, and not looking at what I don't have. We do die, and facing the fear of death is essential. We tend to be so afraid; and while much of this *is* unpleasant, that doesn't have to translate to fear. There are no shortcuts to deep faith. Our Redeemer still lives!"

Kari still knows deep days of discouragement, especially when her body fails and the pain ratchets up. But she insists, "Although the evil one whispers discouraging words into our hearts, we must rebuke that in the name of Jesus Christ and His sacrificed life in His death on the cross. I have found not to be afraid of quietness, because that is when God truly speaks to us. Be silent. Cry out to God until you feel His comfort. We are not alone! Cry when you must."

Like many others I know who have joined the fellowship of the sacred ache, Kari says something surprising that might even shock some people: "Although healing might be nice, looking back, I might not want to trade healing for the intimacy I have with Jesus. I look back and see God's healing presence clearer than ever. My heart is at peace, and that can be only from God."

While I've never heard Kari use the term *sacred ache*, I'm quite sure she knows more about it than I do. Accepting this sacred ache has kept her from extremes, as much from the foolish denial of "everything's fine!" as from the satanic lie of "everything's over!" Her life, as filled with pain and suffering as it continues to be, demonstrates that the sacred ache also has a beautiful side. You might not think so if you saw Kari's ravaged body, but if you looked there, I'd say you had chosen the wrong place. Look rather into her soul, into her Christlike spirit. For there you would find beauty and more every day.

Such is the work of the sacred ache.

A Reminder of What's to Come

In an epilogue written twelve years after the tragic accident that killed three members of his family, Jerry Sittser reckoned that he had changed in three ways.

First, he had changed inwardly, shedding some of the selfishness, ambition, and impatience that he thought had plagued his prior life. Although he still calls himself "the quintessential 'type A' personality," now he lives with more transcendence, freedom, and lightheartedness.

Second, he had exchanged *performing* as a father for *being* a father and has reaped the benefits of a far closer relationship with his three surviving children.[49]

The third change might be the most expansive of all. He discovered that "our lives are part of a greater story. What once seemed chaotic and random, like a deck of cards thrown into the air, has started to look like the plot of a wonderful story. It is not entirely clear yet how things will turn out. But I have lived this story long enough now to know that something extraordinary is unfolding, as if it were an epic that would give Homer a run for his money."[50]

And then he makes a statement that I believe only one who has come to live with the sacred ache can truthfully say:

> I see the course my life has taken as if sitting atop a mountain pass that provides a clear view of where I have come from and where I am going. It may not always be so. But I have this sense that the story God has begun to write he will finish. That story will be good. The accident remains now, as it always has been, a horrible experience that did great damage to us and to so many others. It was and will remain a very bad chapter. But the whole of my life is becoming what appears to be a very good book. [51]

Sacred aches have a way of giving us a new and heavenly perspective that transforms the way we see and experience life. As Paul wrote to the church in Rome, "For his Spirit joins with our spirit to affirm that we are God's children. And since we are his children, we are his heirs. In fact, together with Christ we are heirs of God's glory. But if we are to share his glory, we must also share his suffering. Yet what we suffer now is nothing compared to the glory he will reveal to us later" (Romans 8:16–18 NLT).

Our suffering, surrendered to God, transforms common earthly ground. It has done this for Jerry, it has done this for Kari, and it has done this for me.

A Vision of What Always Remains True

About two years ago I sat in a packed arena with fifteen thousand women singing together—and yet I felt a deep sadness, an ache inside. I asked the Lord, "Why do I still feel this way sometimes? When will this be done?"

While I am not given to visions or to hearing the audible voice of God, what happened to me that day was a gift that I carry with me everywhere I go. As I prayed, it seemed that in that moment I sensed myself in a different place. The arena and the crowds disappeared, and I stood at an open door to a great room inside a castle. I knew the figure seated on the chair was Christ, and He beckoned me to come in. I went to Him, knelt at His feet, and laid my head on His lap. He placed one hand on my head and held the other up, as if to stop anyone else from coming in.

I don't remember hearing His voice, but I clearly understood His message. This sacred ache that burdened me wasn't something to despise or run from, but a reminder of where I am now and where I am going—as if the DNA of Eden, buried deep inside, reminded me of *more* awaiting us, so much more.

I also sensed Jesus telling me that when the ache becomes too much to bear, I should look for Him in a quiet place where I can unfailingly find a place to rest my head. And Christ will keep the world at bay.

All of the words of this chapter come down to this: Let Jesus turn your pain into a sacred ache! Let it enlarge your soul rather than shrink your life. And on those days when that ache grows too strong to bear, let your head fall into the lap of your Savior, Jesus Christ, the Good Shepherd.

Remember, it's the Shepherd's job—not ours—to get us home.

THIRTEEN

CHRIST THE BROKEN
The Savior Who Chose Suffering . . . for You

How many times over the course of your life have you participated in the Lord's Supper? You might call it Communion, or maybe the Eucharist—but how often have you taken the sacred bread and eaten it as you heard the ancient words recited, "This is My body, broken for you"?

Since birth I have sat in churches around the world and either watched or taken part in this holy remembrance of the Last Supper, when Jesus prepared His disciples one final time for the agonies of the passion to come. I cannot count the number of times I have partaken of the bread and the wine (or as often as not, crackers and grape juice) in my more than five decades on this planet.

But how often I have partaken of this meal isn't really a very important statistic, is it? What really counts isn't how often but rather, what did those Communion moments actually mean to me—and to Him? How many times did I receive the Lord's Supper while *really pondering* the meaning of those awesome words, "This is My body, broken for you"? How often have I swallowed the bread and downed the wine while thinking, *I hope that chicken I put in the oven to roast is okay*, or something equally shallow?

I thought about all of that as I prepared to write this final chapter. And I wondered if it would help me to more deeply appreciate Christ's broken body on my behalf if I imagined He had never come. It isn't a pleasant mental journey to even let my thoughts drift in this direction. But it may be something I very well need to do. What if I lived in a doubly cursed world in which the Christ of Christmas never arrived—*but someone else turned up instead*?

It's the un-Christmas story.

And it is also a nightmare.

Long, long ago in a universe far, far away, a newborn baby cried out in the night. His sinfully rich parents, rulers over the most powerful kings on earth, directed the child's anxious nannies to wrap him in the finest silk and place him in a solid gold cradle. A hundred-voice choir, handpicked for the occasion, sang softly in the background to soothe the baby to sleep, as a large contingent of slaves worked furiously to stoke the palace furnace to ensure the infant felt no drafts.

"No one is to disturb the prince," the parents warned their frightened slaves. "Make sure the people know the penalty for interrupting his slumber." No one wanted *this* rich baby to awake, and certainly no crying to make. The slaves shot a furtive glance out the window and saw the long row of gallows erected just outside the palace grounds, and quaked once more. Ten of their number already had swung in the breeze as "examples," and the lesson had not gone unlearned.

A strange hole in the sky seemed to hover above the child's nursery, sucking the light from the stars and bathing the whole royal enclave in a murky, almost palpable darkness. "Already he rules the night," chuckled the boy's father. "Truly he is the Prince."

Even as he spoke, the learned and mighty of the land hurriedly made their way to the palace to honor this long-expected Prince with gifts of rubies, rose water, and mint. In their fear and haste, they scattered scores of feeble peasants along the road, lashing them with whips and cursing them with shouts of, "Out of the way, vermin! We have urgent business in Bet Meihem!" One group of shepherds did not move quickly enough and got trampled beneath the hooves of a caravan laden with precious tribute. Pieces of their bodies lay strewn upon the earth. "Good! We'll to men our power make known," sneered one rider as he galloped off into the blackness.

As the screams of dying men trailed off into a deathly silent night, no joy came to this world, for its Lord had come. And neither heaven nor nature would sing again for a very, very long time.

I shudder to think of such a ghastly world, ruled not by the Prince of Peace but by the Prince of Darkness. Do we marvel anymore that Christ came into our world, not as a pampered royal, but as a poor peasant's son? Do our souls quake with deepest joy and gratitude that even in His arrival, He chose to identify with the broken, the beleaguered, and the beaten down? Excited shepherds followed angelic directions to worship at the infant's manger, and a mysterious "star" pointed unwelcome foreign dignitaries to the child's home.

Do we notice that, from the very beginning, this beautiful Savior of ours came to the broken that He might be utterly broken Himself?

Pastor and author Tim Keller has said, "If you believe in Christmas—that God became a human being—you have an ability to face suffering, a resource for suffering that others don't have. We sometimes wonder why God doesn't just end suffering. But we know that whatever the reason, it isn't one of indifference or remoteness. God so hates suffering and evil that He was willing to come into it and become enmeshed in it."[52] And Dorothy Sayers said of Jesus, "He was born in poverty and died in disgrace and thought it well worthwhile."[53]

How much of all this do we ponder when on a bright Sunday morning we eat the sacred bread and hear the familiar words, "This is My body, broken for you"? What would it take for us to remember?

Communion with Nothing

Some twenty-five years ago a hurting old man with a thick accent stood up in front of a seminary audience and announced he wanted to talk about nothing.

Richard Wurmbrand, a Lutheran pastor with a Jewish heritage, spent fourteen excruciating years in a Romanian prison. In his famous book titled *Tortured for Christ*, he described how he spent many of those years thirty feet below the surface of the earth, confined all alone in a bare, gray cell. He and other Christians had become the targets of his nation's Communist masters for proclaiming the good news of the broken Christ.

He told the young seminarians that day that his imprisonment lasted so long that he forgot colors even existed; he could imagine nothing but the gray of his cell wall and uniform. He lost track of time, of day and night, of the seasons. For fourteen years he saw not a single woman, child, butterfly, or bird. He never received a smile or even a single nod of affirmation.

"We were in prison, and we were forsaken," he said. "We were hungry after some sign that we were loved by somebody in the world."

Wurmbrand and his friends also faced aching physical hunger. "There were times when we had one slice of bread a week, otherwise super dirty

potato peels, cabbage with unwashed intestines, and other such dainties,"
he told the hushed audience. "There were beatings, there were tortures.
During fourteen years . . . we have never seen a Bible or any other book. We
never had any writing material."

They lived in an utterly gray, utterly solitary, utterly dismal world.

Sometime later, when he and the others got transferred to slave labor
camps, they saw a bird stuck in barbed wire. "She probably had flown; it was
a young bird, she was not attentive, and she was caught in the barbed wire,"
Wurmbrand recalled. "And would you believe that other birds came and
freed her from the barbed wire! Some pushed from down, and some pulled
from above, and they took her out from the barbed wire. And we were
behind barbed wire, and nobody came to take us out. We had the feeling that
we were forgotten and abandoned by everyone."

Although the prisoners confined in their underground cells could not see
each other or speak directly with one another, they did know of each other's
existence. Somehow they taught each other Morse code and communicated
with one another by lightly banging on the pipes of their prison. In this way
they discovered that many of them felt an intense hunger for something else.

"There was one hunger more which is not known in America,"
Wurmbrand said, "the hunger after Holy Communion. Years had passed,
and we had not taken Holy Communion. And we knew the words of our Lord
about Holy Communion, 'you should do this in remembrance of Me, and
who does not eat My flesh and does not drink My blood, has no part with
Me.' And years had passed without Holy Communion."

But what could they do? At that time, Wurmbrand recalled, "we had no
bread at all. Instead of bread, they gave us a dirty rice cake. We had no Bible,
we had no hymnal, we had nothing. And we wished to take Holy Communion.
But how could we take Holy Communion when we had nothing? Nothing!
We had nothing, and we were nothing. They put us forcibly on the floor, they
opened the mouths of Christians, forcibly, and spit in their mouths. I will
not say more, but there were worse things than that. We were nothing. And
we had nothing."

How could these broken men fulfill such a holy longing *with nothing*?
They continued to dream of participating in the Lord's Supper, but with no
notion of how to turn their dream into reality. Finally, one prisoner had an
idea—a peculiar, odd, irrationally brilliant idea.

"Well, we are not poor," the man tapped out in Morse. "We have some-thing. You said it yourself, through Morse. We have nothing. If nothing really were nothing, we could not have it. You can have only something. Therefore we have something which is called nothing. Now, what is the value of nothing?"

Wurmbrand thought, *What do you mean, what is the value of nothing?*

"Think of this beautiful earth," the man continued, "with five billion people on it, and with forests and with oceans, animals and birds. And out of what did God make this world? Out of nothing! So we have a valuable material, out of which a world has been made. Nothing is something! If anyone would try to make such a world out of gold or diamonds, he would not succeed. But out of nothing, such a world is made."

The man continued, "Secondly, it is written in Job 26 that God hung this earth, this huge ball, upon nothing. If he would have hung the earth upon a thick cable of steel, the thick cable of steel would have broken. But nothing does not break. The world has hung on nothing for millions of years. So we have a very valuable material, and we have the most resistant material of all."

Suddenly another man remembered what St. Paul had written to the Corinthians: "In his time there were quarrels in the church. Some said Paul—he was unsurpassed. Others said, 'Go away. You have not heard Peter preaching. Peter puts Paul in his small pocket.' And others said, 'You should hear Apollos. He's the real one.' And because all three preached love, instead of loving each other, they quarreled with each other about who is the better preacher. And then Paul writes to them, 'I am nothing.' *Nothing*.

"Now, Billy Graham is considered to be the biggest soul winner in this century. All respect for him, he is a very big preacher. But he also will agree with me, that Paul is a little bit bigger than he. And about Billy Graham it is written that he is a big preacher; about St. Paul, he has another title: 'I am nothing.' To be nothing is something more than to be a big preacher. And so we have this title, of being nothing, of having nothing. Why would we not take Holy Communion with nothing?"

Wurmbrand then explained to his rapt audience that although he opposed any innovation in theology—once our Lord has brought a revelation, we need nobody to add to it or modify it—he and his fellow prisoners found themselves in exceptional circumstances. So one Sunday, "a signal was given from one end of the corridor to the other end of the prison cells, at one and the same moment, every Christian took in his hands nothing. Together we thanked God for the nothing we had, and then we blessed nothing."

They blessed nothing? What does that mean?

"You must not have a thing to bless," Wurmbrand explained. "You bless because blessings flow from you. Electricity must not have something to electrify. It is just electricity. And blessings flow from a man. So we blessed nothing."

At a signal, the men all broke nothing together. "And it is so easy to break nothing!" Wurmbrand declared. "I belong to the Lutheran church, and in the Lutheran church you take Holy Communion, not with bread but with oblate, if you know what is such round thing. And when you break them, they make, 'Poch!' They oppose the resistance. But nothing opposes no resistance. 'He was taken to the slaughter like a lamb, and did not resist.' We ate nothing, and we remembered the body of our Lord Jesus Christ, which has been broken for us."

At yet another signal the prisoners took another nothing. "Nothings can be of many kinds," Wurmbrand said with a smile. "A car can be only of a certain brand. If it is a Toyota, it is not a Volkswagen; if it's a Volkswagen, it is surely not a Rolls Royce. It is one certain kind. But nothings can be of so many kinds. And we took a second nothing, and we thanked God for the second nothing. We blessed the second nothing. We drank nothing and we remembered the blood of our Lord Jesus Christ, which has been shed for us."

As Wurmbrand's remarkable story wound to a close, his voice filled with emotion and his eyes welled up with tears. "This was one of the most glorious and most beautiful Holy Communion services which I ever attended in my life," he declared. And even though none of the seminary staff and none of the students had attended that "nothing service" so many years before, the looks on their faces showed that his talk on nothing had, perhaps, had more of a profound effect on them than anything.

Broken for You

If you grew up on the King James Version, as I did, the exact "words of the institution" for the Lord's Supper go like this: "Take, eat: this is my body, which is broken for you: this do in remembrance of me" (1 Corinthians 11:24).

The past few days I've been thinking a lot about the Lord's Supper and pondering what it means, not only in general, but to me personally. What does it mean that I, Sheila Walsh, a broken person, have a Savior who allowed wicked men to break His own body—for *me*?

My mind travels back to the Last Supper itself. As Jesus gathered His closest friends around Him, *He* took the bread and *He* broke it. The bread didn't come pre-broken or neatly segmented, as ours often does. Nor did He ask Peter or John or one of the other disciples to break the bread for Him.

He did it Himself, with His own two hands, in His own time.

Jesus therefore declares that, unlike me, He *chose* brokenness. He who existed from eternity past in an unbroken state chose to be broken—for me. "I lay down my life—only to take it up again," Jesus had told His disciples. "No one takes it from me, but I lay it down of my own accord" (John 10:17–18).

As Jesus took the bread in His hands and broke it, what did He feel? What did He think? We know what He said: "Take and eat; this is my body" (Matthew 26:26). Through these symbolic actions He taught us that He would voluntarily lay down His life for us, so that we might live through Him as we become a part of Him. Every time we eat the Communion bread, His broken body, we depict with tangible things the intangible trust we have placed in Him for our eternal salvation.

But I have a confession to make.

Something happened after the Supper, in fact during and after the crucifixion, that used to bother me. It may not seem like a big thing to you, and probably it's not. And yet it has pricked at my brain for many years nonetheless. I had a hard time reconciling Jesus' words about His broken body with a prophecy that John went to great lengths to highlight.

Here's the passage I found a bit, well, troublesome:

Now it was the day of Preparation, and the next day was to be a special Sabbath. Because the Jews did not want the bodies left on the crosses during the Sabbath, they asked Pilate to have the legs broken and the bodies taken down. The soldiers therefore came and broke the legs of the first man who had been crucified with Jesus, and then those of the other. But when they came to Jesus and found that he was already dead, they did not break his legs. Instead, one of the soldiers pierced Jesus' side with a spear, bringing a sudden flow of blood and water. The man who saw it has given testimony, and his testimony is true. He knows that he tells the truth, and he testifies so that you also may believe. These things happened so that the scripture would be fulfilled: "Not one of his bones will be broken," and, as another scripture says, "They will look on the one they have pierced." (John 19:31–37)

You may think I'm being too picky about the actual words used, but it felt somehow unsettling to me that while Jesus would emphasize His broken body, John would emphasize His *un*broken bones. The two just didn't seem in sync to me. Broken or unbroken? Which was it?

Over the years I have come to understand how the horrifying abuse of Jesus—His beating, torture, and execution—more than qualifies Him as "broken." If you saw the 2004 film *The Passion of the Christ*, you know how difficult it can be to get those ghastly images of suffering out of your mind. Yes, Jesus was broken! Broken as none of us ever will be.

And yet why did John want to focus on the fact that our Lord died with His bones intact? Why did this seem so important to him? Despite how silly my old misgivings might have been, I don't consider this a silly question. I have discovered three reasons I believe John emphasized this detail.

The first and most obvious is the one John himself supplies: "These things happened so that the scripture would be fulfilled." John had in mind one Bible text explicitly and two implicitly. The explicit prophecy comes from Psalm 34:20, which commentators even prior to the New Testament considered a messianic psalm. The verse reads, "He protects all his bones, not one of them will be broken." The two implied verses come from Exodus 12:46 and Numbers 9:12, both of which stipulate that the Passover lamb must be sacrificed without breaking any of its bones. Since the New Testament calls Jesus our Passover Lamb (1 Corinthians 5:7), John saw it as crucial that none of His bones be broken—and they weren't.

I used to see this point merely as an intellectual assurance that Bible prophecy confirms Jesus as the Messiah. Today I see it as much more. Broken people need to know that God keeps His word, even down to the smallest detail. So many of us have watched lies destroy our homes and broken promises shatter our lives. But this seemingly minor guarantee that God would allow no one to break the Messiah's bones shouts to me that I can trust Him in all things, both the big and the small. And therefore I glory in the words of Paul: "For no matter how many promises God has made, they are 'Yes' in Christ" (2 Corinthians 1:20). Because I am "in Christ," the Bible's promises are all "yes" for me. And if you are in Christ, then they are "yes" for you too!

The second reason goes a little deeper. We ought to ask, *why* did God forbid the ancient Hebrews from breaking the bones of the Passover lamb? There appear to be two possible answers. First, if you don't break any of the lamb's bones, then you keep it intact, and all the members of your household clearly eat from the same lamb. In the Exodus, God created a single nation, the chosen people; and eating from an unbroken lamb signified their unity. Second, Exodus 12:5 stipulated that the Passover lamb be a male, without defect; a broken bone would disqualify it and make it defective.

As our Passover Lamb, Jesus connects us to God and to each other through the pure, spotless, and perfect sacrifice of Himself. Faith in Christ connects you in a living way to the entire body of Christ, meaning that despite how you might feel in your times of deep pain, you are *never* really alone. More than that, since you belong to Christ by faith, God sees you as He sees His own spotless Son—He regards you as without defect, perfect, and therefore invites you to come freely into His holy presence, without fear and without the slightest tinge of guilt.

Peter declared we have been redeemed "with the precious blood of Christ, a lamb without blemish or defect," and therefore we no longer have to remain stuck in "the empty way of life" handed down to us by other broken people (1 Peter 1:18–19). Never forget that just as God accepted completely the perfect sacrifice of Christ, so in Christ He accepts you completely and perfectly. Forever!

The third reason may go even a little deeper still. Remember that as sunset approached and Jesus' body remained on the cross, the Romans intended to break His legs. They did this as a matter of custom, to hasten the deaths of those crucified. When the soldiers came to the three crosses described in the Gospels, they did break the legs of the two thieves crucified on either side of Jesus. When they came to Jesus, He was already dead. Why go to the trouble of breaking a dead man's bones?

To make sure He had expired, they pierced His side with a spear and immediately blood and water poured out—a sure sign of death, since the blood of the deceased begins to separate into its constituent parts. Jesus had died when He dismissed His spirit into the care of His heavenly Father (Luke 23:46), demonstrating that even in death, He showed Himself to be in total control.

Broken people need to remember this!

When we suffer, when tragedy stalks us or hardship overwhelms us, we tend to think that events have spun out of God's control, or that our pain proves He doesn't love us, has forgotten us, or is ignoring us. But Jesus' unbroken bones tell me that God remains in control, even when events seem to scream otherwise. The Romans, the undisputed rulers of the Mediterranean, *intended* to break Jesus' legs.

But they didn't.

And they never would.

God said, "Thus far, and no farther." It was as if He declared, "Yes, you can break Him; but you can't break His bones."

Do you remember when Jesus told His followers that, after His death, men would lay hands on them, persecute them, jail them, even kill them because of their connection to Christ? And yet, Jesus said, "But not a hair of your head will perish" (Luke 21:18).

What an odd passage. *You might be jailed, beaten, or executed, but you won't lose so much as a single hair.* What in the world does that mean?

Now, it's possible to read this verse in a way that gives no comfort at all. I mean, it doesn't sound all that comforting that we can all die with a full head of hair (unless you're already bald, in which case you're *really* up the creek without a hairbrush). But that is to badly misread the verse.

Jesus means two very important things in this statement.

First, the eternal life God has given to you is beyond the reach of man, and no one can touch it.

Second, God Himself sets limits on the amount of brokenness He allows into each believer's life.

While each case differs from every other case, no case ever spins out of His control. *Whatever* God allows, He always remains in control. He has not forgotten you, misplaced your file, sent your desperate heart cry to voice mail, or given you partial attention while His mind was really elsewhere. No, our breaking has a divinely appointed limit: "Thus far, and no farther."

'When I Survey the Wondrous Cross

In the fall of 2011, as I was finishing this book, I was also preparing to go into a Nashville studio to record a CD, *Beauty from Ashes*. Often I cowrite songs with other musicians who know me well; but sometimes I am reminded of an old song or discover a new one that was written by someone else that so connects with my heart that I just *have* to include it.

As the songs came together, I found it hard to ignore that the book and the music told the same story—that God loves broken people, even those who pretend they're not or wish they weren't. I had one slot left on the CD, and I chose a hymn I have sung since I was a child. It also reminded me of one of the most beautiful Communion services I have ever had the privilege of leading.

My mother-in-law, Eleanor, was dying. Barry, Christian, and I had moved into my in-laws' home in Charleston, South Carolina, to help my father-in-law, William, care for her. Late one night all the boys had fallen asleep. Just before she left, the hospice nurse told me that she believed it would only be a matter of a few days. I locked the door after her and came back into Eleanor's bedroom.

I asked if I could get her anything. She said she was fine and asked if Barry and William were asleep. When I told her they were, she asked, "Did William have communion before he went to bed?" I laughed and assured her that he did. "Communion," as he called it, was my father-in-law's excuse for drinking very cheap port and making it sound holy.

"What's he going to do when I'm gone?" she asked.

"Don't worry, Mom; we'll take care of him," I assured her.

And then a thought occurred to me.

"Mom, would you like us to share Communion?" I asked.

"I'm not drinking that stuff!" she replied.

"No, I don't mean that," I assured her. "I mean sharing together what Christ did for you and for me."

She smiled.

I returned with a saltine cracker (all she could manage by then) and a little ginger ale. I sat on the edge of her bed, broke the cracker, and we ate and drank together. It was the last Communion she ever took. She was so close to crossing the river I could see eternity sparkle in her eyes as I sang,

When I survey the wondrous cross,
On which the Prince of glory died,
My richest gain I count but loss,
And pour contempt on all my pride.

Forbid it, Lord, that I should boast,
Save in the death of Christ my God;
All the vain things that charm me most,
I sacrifice them to His blood.

See from His head, His hands, His feet,
Sorrow and love flow mingled down;
Did e'er such love and sorrow meet,
Or thorns compose so rich a crown?

Were the whole realm of nature mine,
That were a present far too small;
Love so amazing, so divine,
Demands my soul, my life, my all.

Communion with a saltine cracker and ginger ale. Communion with nothing. What does it matter? So long as it is true Communion with Christ the Broken—broken for you and broken for me—it leaves us changed, marked by His shed blood forever.

To be broken is to follow in Christ's footsteps. But to embrace it is to follow His heart.

EPILOGUE

Longing for Eden

> If I find in myself a desire which no experience in this world can satisfy,
> the most probable explanation is that I was made for another world.
>
> —C. S. LEWIS, *MERE CHRISTIANITY*

We dream of Eden—of Paradise—because we don't have it here. Not in Hawaii, not in Tahiti, not in Monte Carlo, not in the loveliest, most charming places you have ever visited on this planet.

Of all the humans who have ever lived, only two experienced the complete peace and beauty of Eden, and their disobedience made it impossible for them to stay for very long.

That garden is gone, or perhaps hidden from our eyes until all things are renewed.

And yet the desire remains.

In a sense, much of this book has focused on the attempt to balance our true and right and legitimate desire for Paradise (God made us for it, after all) with our decidedly non-Edenic experience on this warped planet, so horribly disfigured by the disease of sin.

It isn't an easy balance to find.

Who doesn't want Paradise? But our frantic attempts to get it *right now*, on this broken world, almost inevitably set us up for disappointment, discouragement, depression, and often, feelings of deep desolation.

So what are we to do? Hunker down, curl up in a ball, and just wait for better days to come? Pretend that what God promises for our future has already arrived and so paste on a happy face? Self-medicate our pain with a witch's brew of drugs, alcohol, sex, conspicuous consumption, and whatever else seems to dull the pain for a moment? Adopt the ancient playboy philosophy, "Let us eat, drink, and be merry, for tomorrow we die"?

As you might have guessed, I don't think so.

A far more productive, healthy, upbeat, and satisfying formula comes from the pen of Dag Hammarskjöld, who served as United Nations Secretary General from 1953 to 1961. After his death at age fifty-six in a mysterious plane crash in the Congo (where he was pursuing yet another peace mission), researchers found a fascinating line he'd written in his personal journal.

He wrote the line to God. Here it is:

"For everything that has been, thank you, and for everything that will be, yes!"

As a two-term secretary general of the United Nations, Hammarskjöld saw more than his share of this world's pain and suffering. Yet he tirelessly sought to alleviate as much of that pain as he could, right up to the moment of his death. He is still the only person ever to win a Nobel Peace Prize posthumously. How did he keep going?

For everything that has been, thank You, and for everything that will be, yes!

Hammarskjöld cultivated the twin habits of thankfulness and joyful submission to God's agenda—whatever that agenda might entail.

Could we do the same thing? As we long for Paradise while living in this broken world, could we, like Dag Hammarskjöld, give thanks to God for what He already has done even as we make up our minds to joyfully accept whatever He brings next? I don't claim it's easy. Although Hammarskjöld had no way of knowing it, he said yes to the plane crash that ultimately took his life. If you could interview him now, would he still say yes? Having read much of what he wrote about his spiritual journey, I believe that he would. He trusted not in *what* he might be saying yes to, but rather he trusted the One to whom he said yes!

I know the apostle Paul would as well. In his final letter before his execution, just four verses before the last sentence he ever wrote, he declared, "The Lord will rescue me from every evil attack and will bring me safely to his heavenly kingdom. To him be glory forever and ever. Amen" (2 Timothy 4:18). Paul, too, longed for Eden—or something even better. I wonder how often he sang the words of the psalmist:

> *My soul yearns, even faints,*
> *for the courts of the Lord;*
> *my heart and my flesh cry out*
> *for the living God.*

Even the sparrow has found a home,
and the swallow a nest for herself,
where she may have her young—
a place near your altar,
Lord Almighty, my King and my God.

(Psalm 84:2–3)

If you have a song in your heart like *that*, then you have within your spirit the sort of power and grace that enabled both Dag Hammarskjöld and the apostle Paul to pen the kinds of lines that still give hope to broken people like me.

No, it isn't easy.

But in this world, why *should* it be?

After all, "we have this treasure in jars of clay to show that this all-surpassing power is from God and not from us" (2 Corinthians 4:7).

I'll never forget the night that my father-in-law, William, suffered a fatal heart attack. I anxiously followed the ambulance that carried him to the hospital. After I learned he had died, I asked to see his body—and instantly it became so clear that all that remained was the shell. The real William had left, leaving behind only the jar of clay.

I found myself wondering that night, *Why do we spend so much time worrying about the presentability of the jar, when what really matters is the treasure contained within?*

You are a treasure, whether you feel like it or not.

God loves you and has something better than Paradise planned for you, whether you sense it or not.

When you place your trust in Jesus, your story will end very, *very* well, whether you can believe that right now or not.

That's what has changed me on this journey. It seems to me now that it is through the window of my brokenness that I see the face of God. I used to only see my own reflection in the glass, what was wrong, unlovely, and weak. But when God in His fierce and fiery love allowed the walls of my glass cage to smash and splinter . . . I saw Him. Fixing my gaze on Him has changed everything. It's not that I have become a stronger believer, but rather that in my weakness, Christ has proved Himself strong over and over again. So although I will be a bummer lamb until the day I get home, I know whose I am and I know that the Shepherd has committed Himself to get me, to get you, all the way home!

And so I invite you to join me in the prayer of Dag Hammarskjöld . . . and into the adventure and the promise it suggests:

For everything that has been, thank You, and for everything that will be, yes!

Acknowledgments

It felt like a long, drawn-out fight to get this book written, but I am very aware that I was not alone in the ring. I'd like to thank those who stood shoulder by shoulder with me.

Brian Hampton, thank you for the grace and space to get it right. You could have called this one—but you let us go for as many rounds as we needed to.

Bryan Norman, what can I say? You continue to give me a place to grow, and you cheer when I get it right and listen when it feels wrong. You are so much more than a great editor. You are a great friend.

Christin Ditchfield, thank you for allowing yourself to get a little bloodied in this battle. You provided so much encouragement to me when I know you needed it too. Your insights were great, but your heart even greater.

Lee Hough and Rick Christian, every fighter needs someone who will be their champion, and you stepped into the ring when I was down for the count and picked me up. I am deeply grateful.

Steve Halliday, what a blast it has been to work side by side with you! I love your wit and wisdom, your way with words and heart of wonder at the fiery love of God. I have learned so much from working with you; thank you.

Larry Libby, you have such a gift of understanding the nuances of language. You polish each word until it shines like a prizefighter's belt!

Barry and Christian Walsh, the encouragement and love I receive from both of you are unrelenting. You anchor me in the shaky seasons of life, and I love you.

O N E

I'm Not Waving; I'm Drowning

When Deep Water Meets Even Deeper Love

Broken Pieces

- 1. Define in your own words what it means to be broken.
- 2. Reflecting on your own life, which describes you more accurately? Explain what this looks like for you under the appropriate statement.

I have struggled with admitting to myself and others I'm broken.

_____

I know I'm broken, but have struggled with how to deal with it.

_____

- 3. Sheila quotes Stevie Smith's poem, "I was much too far out all my life/ And not waving but drowning." Write down your own drowning experience. How did you survive?

Restored Vessels

Brokenness can be realized in our lives in different ways. Sometimes it is a conviction about sin that breaks us. At other times we are paralyzed in the realization of our weakness or what we lack. Both kinds of brokenness point to our need for divine help. Both scenarios prove that our human condition limits us.

As we study what the Bible teaches us about brokenness, let's begin with the obvious source of our brokenness, sin. From a biblical perspective, sin is something that alienates us from God. It is the act of wrongdoing that ruptures our relationship with God. We become aware of our sinfulness when we are confronted with a holy God.

Paul uses the Greek word *hamartia* to describe sin that is not just a willful sin but a debilitating enmity with God. Throughout his letters to the church, it is clear that Paul understands at a very deep level that the wages of sin is death. Sin holds us as prisoners, threatening our relationship with Him. None of us is alone as Romans 3:23 reminds us that all have sinned and fallen short. So we can take comfort—all of us need a Savior!

Hamartia is also derived in part from the Greek understanding of tragedy, which is also linked to the word *hubris*. Most of us understand hubris in terms of pride. In ancient Greek culture, hubris equated to trying to rise to the level of the gods, to live as superhuman. So sin is an attempt to elevate ourselves to a godlike status, and we try to defy sin by overcompensating with our abilities.

For followers of Jesus, the core understanding of sin is unbelief, which is closely associated with hardness of heart. We sometimes are too stubborn to open our hearts to the love of God.

- 4. What do the following verses say about sin and how God's people respond?

    Isaiah 6:5
    Psalm 51:1–9
    Luke 5:8

    I have often found anger more comfortable than fear. Anger gives me the illusion of control, while fear leaves me naked and exposed.
    —Sheila

- 5. When we are faced with conflict, it is easy for our sin nature to react We tend to go where our comfort zone is, whether that is to respond in anger or to retreat in self-pity. What does your "sin comfort zone" look like?

Read Psalm 88 (ESV)

O Lord, God of my salvation;
I cry out day and night before you.

²*Let my prayer come before you;*
incline your ear to my cry!

³*For my soul is full of troubles,*
and my life draws near to Sheol.
⁴*I am counted among those who go*
      down to the pit;
I am a man who has no strength,
⁵*like one set loose among the dead,*
like the slain that lie in the grave,
like those whom you remember no
      more,
for they are cut off from your hand.
⁶*You have put me in the depths of the*
      pit,
in the regions dark and deep.
⁷*Your wrath lies heavy upon me,*
and you overwhelm me with all
      your waves.
Selah

⁸*You have caused my companions to*
      shun me;
you have made me a horror to them.
I am shut in so that I cannot escape;
⁹ *my eye grows dim through sorrow.*
Every day I call upon you, O Lord;
I spread out my hands to you.
¹⁰*Do you work wonders for the dead?*
Do the departed rise up to praise you?
Selah

¹¹*Is your steadfast love declared in the*
      grave,
or your faithfulness in Abaddon?
¹²*Are your wonders known in the*
      darkness,

or your righteousness in the land of
forgetfulness?

¹³But I, O LORD, cry to you;
in the morning my prayer comes before
you.
¹⁴O LORD, why do you cast my soul
away?
Why do you hide your face from me?
¹⁵Afflicted and close to death from my
youth up,
I suffer your terrors; I am helpless.
¹⁶Your wrath has swept over me;
your dreadful assaults destroy me.
¹⁷They surround me like a flood all day
long;
they close in on me together.
¹⁸You have caused my beloved and my
friend to shun me;
my companions have become darkness.

- 6. In the right column next to the psalm, personalize each paragraph to reflect your prayer and confession to God.

Stepping-Stones

When we're under the weight of brokenness, it can be hard to reach out to God. The energy it takes to lift our heads to heaven seems impossible. In the midst of brokenness, our faith in God must hold on to His promise to deliver. The psalmist above confesses his perpetual anguish as he shouts for divine help. In his torment, he calls for help every day, even in the depths of despair.

- 7. Though the psalm ends in lament, how does it show faith in God?

Two

Bummer Lambs and Black Sheep
A Shepherd Who Pursues Both Victims and Villains

Broken Pieces

In the case of the ewe on Sharon's farm, a sheep that cannot produce enough milk for multiple offspring will choose to feed some and reject others. These abandoned, rejected lambs are called "bummer lambs." In a spiritual sense, we are all bummer lambs.

Then there are the black sheep, the ones who choose to leave the Good Shepherd. Maybe you have recently chosen to go your own way; you are tired of waiting on God. Rebellion has taken a grip on your heart, and you can't seem to find your way back because you aren't sure if you deserve His grace.

- 1. Do you most identify with the bummer lamb or the black sheep?

    "He brought me out into a spacious place; he rescued me because he delighted in me." (Psalm 18:19)

- 2. Write down the benefits of being a bummer lamb shared in the chapter.

    In a spiritual sense, we're all "bummer lambs"—lost in sin, broken in spirit, wounded in heart and mind . . . and sometimes body. Many of us have felt like bummer lambs in our family of origin, or even (sad to say) in the family of God. We know what it means to feel unwanted and unloved, pushed out of the way, abandoned, rejected, abused, or neglected.

    p. 16

Restored Vessels

Referring back to chapter 2, write out the definition for the Hebrew word *chavash*:

- 3. In light of this word, fill in the blank. My Shepherd, Jesus, has
  _____ my wounds.

Read John 10:1–21.

This passage resembles Matthew 18:12–14 and Luke 15:3–7, but the John account uses the allegory of shepherd with a wider meaning. The focus is on what the shepherd does for his sheep to create a picture of our relationship as Christ, the Shepherd, and His people, the sheep.

In verses 1–2, Jesus uses the imagery of a sheep pen. In the time of His earthly ministry, this was a structure usually made of rough stones or mudbricks only partially roofed. Sometimes a cave in the hills was used. There was one opening that the shepherd guarded against thieves or wild animals. Thieves tried to access a sheep's pen by other means. Jesus contrasts this by emphasizing the right entry the Good Shepherd uses. False messiahs violated the lawful entry, trying to harm God's people.

- 4. Write out some of the roles of the shepherd mentioned in the text.
- 5. John 10:4 says that the shepherd walks ahead of his sheep and they follow him because they know his voice. Take several minutes to reflect on a time when it was clear God was leading you every step of the way, going before you. Recall His faithfulness, how He revealed His love and character. Remember yourself during this time too. How did you interact with people and make decisions? How did you interact with God?

Jesus used the metaphor of a shepherd because this was very common occupation in Palestine. Throughout the Old Testament we see figurative and allegorical references to the occupation of shepherd. Abel is the first shepherd mentioned in the Bible (Genesis 4:2). Jesus links His divine nature to the most common occupation known to the biblical world. But the passage closes with the listeners not comprehending Jesus' point because of their spiritual arrogance. They were trusting in their lineage to Abraham, not Jesus as Messiah.

- 6. Why is trust in the Good Shepherd for bummer lambs and black sheep essential?
- 7. Name some tangible blocks in your mind, heart, and personal history that keep you from trusting fully that Jesus can carry you to safe pastures.

If you study the Gospel accounts, you'll find the story of the sheep in Luke as well, with one interesting difference. In Matthew's version, the sheep represents a believer. In Luke's account, the lost sheep stands for a person who comes to faith for the first time. And Jesus says, "There is more joy in heaven over one lost sinner who repents and returns to God than over ninety-nine others who are righteous and haven't strayed away" (Luke 15:7 NLT). Both versions of the story teach us that the Good Shepherd dearly loves *all* of His sheep, whether they have just come to faith or whether they return to Him after a long time of wandering away.

We can take great comfort knowing that Jesus will go after the one lost sheep (Luke 15:3–7) and leave the ninety-nine. This shows His far-reaching compassion for us, even when we choose to stray from His will. Sometimes our desires override our obedience to Him

- 8. What false truths or temptations have you allowed to guide you away from God's truths?

Jesus' main concern was for the salvation of His sheep, access to the abundant life.

Stepping-Stones

The Good Shepherd lays down His life for the sheep, whether you are a black sheep or a bummer lamb. The more time we spend with our Good Shepherd, the more we will hear His voice that says, "I love you as you are, and you belong to Me."

In John 10:7, Jesus said to them again, "I say to you, I am the door of the sheep" (NASB). When the sheep reentered their pen after grazing, the shepherd stood at the door, examining, looking for wounds. He also would make sure nothing harmful entered the pen. After all were accounted for, the door would close.

• 9. Imagine Jesus looking over you. What wounds does He see? Write down the ones that hurt right now in this season of life.

A Closing Prayer

Lord, we trust You with our wounds and our wayward hearts. You know us intimately (John 10:3–5). We know You died for us and laid down Your life for us. Help us, Lord, to not resist Your healing hand. Help us to follow You today with every detail of our lives. We know, Jesus, You are leading us to safe pastures. Amen.

THREE

OLD WOUNDS HAVE GOOD MEMORIES
Finding a Way Out of the Darkness

Broken Pieces

Chapter 3 opens with a confession: "As crazy as it sounds, I believed deep in my heart that this storm was *my* fault, that all of heaven had united in a rage against me. A big part of that misbelief came from a desperate lack of understanding about the true nature of God and His fierce love for me."

It is easy to blame ourselves when life leaves us disappointed. We say things like:

> *Would my husband have stayed if I was prettier?*
> *Did Mom die because I didn't get her the best doctor?*
> *What could I have done? What did I do?*
> *I can't have children, so God must be punishing me.*
> *It must have been my fault.*

• 1. It's important to know ourselves enough to know if shame is keeping us from God. Pray for God to reveal to you any shame that is keeping you from His love. Write down what comes to mind.

> *The difference between guilt and shame is very clear—in theory. We feel guilty for what we do. We feel shame for what we are.*
> —Lewis Smedes

When we take time to ask for forgiveness, God can reveal things we can't see in ourselves at other times. Repentance often comes in our private prayer closets, when we are humble before Him.

- 2. Now prayerfully examine if there is anything God is convicting you to do to reconcile a situation. Complete this short prayer of confession:

"Lord, you have convicted me that I still need to _____.
Give me strength and wisdom so that _____, and
I can receive all the forgiveness you have for me."

Restored Vessels

We see humanity's first encounter with shame in the garden of Eden. The word *shame* first appears in Genesis 2:25: "The man and his wife were both naked, and they felt no shame." The Hebrew word used here is *bosh*, which means to feel insignificant before someone else.

Read Genesis 3

Before the Fall, Adam and Eve didn't have a concept of shame. Their sin caused them to lose their state of innocence. Through the serpent's deception, both Adam and Eve fell into temptation and they disobeyed God. They forfeited paradise, as God had warned them not to eat of the forbidden fruit. The immediate consequence was death and their loss of fellowship with God.

- 3. Compare now Genesis 2:25 and Genesis 3:10. After the Fall, what had changed? What was their reaction to shame?
- 4. In Genesis 3:11, God asks Adam if he had eaten from the tree. What was Adam's response to his obvious shame before God?
- 5. Retrace the account of the Fall. What blessings did Adam and Eve walk in before they knew shame?
- 6. Who did God curse first? What curses followed?

Then the LORD God called to Adam and said to him, "Where are you?"
So he said, "I heard Your voice in the garden, and I was afraid because I was naked; and I hid myself."—Genesis 3:9–10, NKJV

Adam and Eve on trial: Here we are confronted with how holy God is. Before God pronounces His judgment on Adam and Eve, He asks them a series of questions The word *naked* appears repeatedly to communicate the shame they felt that went far beyond what they felt in front of each other. God didn't leave them just shamed in their naked state, but made them garments of animal skin to clothe them. God sacrificed life, the blood of animals, to cover them. Even here we see the provision He made for His children to cover their sin, a foreshadowing of the blood He would shed on the cross.

• 7. Read the following verses. What do they say about what God has done with our shame?
  Psalm 25:2–3
  Romans 9:33
  Romans 10:11
  1 Peter 2:6

It seems that in a world mortally wounded by disobedience and fatally infected with the disease of sin, shame has a role to play in God's redemptive purposes. God intends to use even shame to bring us to Himself, where we can live free of shame forever.

—Sheila, p. 30

Stepping-Stones

• To find the kind of sanctifying shame God intends for our good, consider the following:

1. Say the right things to yourself.
2. Fill your mind with the truth of God's Word.
3. Surround yourself with loving, godly people.

• Fill in blanks below with your own steps toward a balanced view of brokenness.

1. Today, I will tell myself the truth and say:_____
2. I will meditate on the following Scripture:_____
3. I will seek out _____ this week because I know this person encourages me in my faith.

FOUR

RELENTLESS QUESTIONS

His Presence and Peace in Your Darkest Nights and Longest Battles

Broken Pieces

There are many times God declines to answer our *why* questions. The most difficult ones have to do with human suffering:

> *Why did her child get healed and mine died?*
> *Was it my fault?*
> *Should I have had more faith?*
> *Why didn't You save my marriage?*
> *What more could I have done?*
> *Why didn't You stop me from playing the fool?*

- 1. List one of your own *why* questions you've been asking God:

_____

- 2. Why do you think God withholds complete answers sometimes? Read Isaiah 55:8–9.

Restored Vessels

Some of our wrestling with the *whys* can be summed up in the word *theodicy*—coming from the words *theos*, "God," and *dike*, "justice." This term is used to refer to attempts to understand the ways of God with humanity. Part of the discussion is resolved when we appeal to the fact that God is all-powerful, all-loving, and just, despite the reality of evil in the world. And after the garden, the tension of suffering has followed human history. The *why* questions plagued God's people through the Old and New Testaments. Job. David. Jonah. Paul. Mary and Martha. Even Jesus asked His Father, "Why have you forsaken Me?" But when we find our place under God's rule, we cannot ignore who He says He is: All-Powerful. All-Knowing. Loving. Compassionate. Merciful. And Sovereign.

- 3. Reflect a moment on your own suffering you have survived. Has the suffering brought you closer to God or farther away?

Read Matthew 8:5–13, Jesus Heals a Centurion Servant

History of the Centurion Servant: In New Testament times Rome had an elaborate, detailed army. A centurion was a noncommissioned officer who ruled over one hundred men. They were the military backbone, executing orders. His commands were equated to be as authoritative as the emperor himself because his orders were as good as if they came from the emperor. These soldiers didn't have posts in Palestine, but there were auxiliaries under Herod Antipas. The centurion was a non-Jew from outside of Galilee. Jews traditionally hated Roman soldiers for oppressing them.

- 4. What barriers could have kept the Roman soldier from approaching Jesus for help?
- 5. Jesus warned the Jews that their lack of faith in God could keep them from entering the kingdom. We shouldn't overestimate faith— somehow thinking that faith itself is the source of God's goodness – but acknowledge that faith is essentially a bedrock belief in God and what He can do. Why do you think God despises our unbelief?
- 6. Read verse 13. Why was the centurion's servant healed according to the text?
- 7. What did the centurion soldier say to Jesus that would illustrate that he understood how powerful Jesus' authority really was?
  How would you answer these questions raised in chapter 4?

> *How did he get that kind of faith?*
> *What did he know that I don't?*
> *How can I amaze God?*

When our prayers are not answered in the way we want, God still commands us to have faith in Him. The Jews didn't want to hear that this Roman Gentile was welcome at God's banquet table, though it was prophesied in Isaiah 25:6–9. The centurion's faith showed he had a revelation into the nature of Jesus' person and His authority given to Him from God that went beyond the Jewish audience.

Read John 11:1–44.

The story of Lazarus is one of the most remarkable stories we have, and John is the only gospel that records it. This account shows the anguish and pain of two sisters who dearly loved their brother, Lazarus, and who also dearly loved Jesus. They knew Jesus was the only One to help their sick brother. But when He was four days too late, according to their worldly perspective, the *why* began to consume them. They knew He could have come earlier, could have healed him before he died. Jesus also shows His compassion, as verse 35 says, "Jesus wept."

· 8. Why did Jesus wait, according to verse 4 and verse 40?

> *Jesus' faith in His Father's ability to raise Lazarus was so strong, He merely thanked God, as it was good as done. Jesus asked them to roll the stone away. For all those who witnessed this, it would be very hard for anyone to doubt the authority Jesus was given when Lazarus walked out alive again.*

Stepping-Stones

In the case of Mary and Martha, the *why* is somewhat clear by the end of the story. God allowed Lazarus to die so that it might bring Him more glory. Death called for a bigger God, a bigger miracle. As in the case of Mary and Martha, loss can keep us from taking in the power of God and what He can do to redeem a situation.

Romans 8:38–39 says:

I am convinced that nothing can ever separate us from God's love. Neither death nor life, neither angels nor demons, neither our fears for today nor

our worries about tomorrow—not even the powers of hell can separate us
from God's love. No power in the sky above or in the earth below—indeed,
nothing in all creation will ever be able to separate us from the love of God
that is revealed in Christ Jesus our Lord. (NLT)

Perhaps you are in the midst of a profound kind of suffering and the
why threatens to keep you from raising up your shield of faith to testify,
"There is no God more powerful than mine. I trust Him."

My human heart and mind can't understand God's ways, but I trust His
heart. And I have had to fight a hard-won, bloodied war to get to this
place of rest.

—Sheila, pg. 53

· 9. As you wait on God for an answer, anticipate how the wait might bring
Him more glory. Write down your insights.

FIVE

HIDING, PRETENDING, AND OTHER FAILED ESCAPES

Avoiding an Old Strategy That Never Works

Broken Pieces

We all wear masks in one way or another. It's our way of trying to fit in, to belong. The more broken we feel inside, the more we feel compelled to hide our brokenness from others so that they don't laugh at us or reject us. Over the last sixteen years I've spoken to more than four million women from the platform at Women of Faith. I hear the same things over and over:

"I don't like the way I look."
"I don't like the way I feel."
"I hate what I see in the mirror."
"If people knew the real me, no one would want to know me."

· 1. Think about the various circles where you spend most of your time. Circle the settings below where you feel like you can be yourself and not wear any kind of mask. Add other social settings that might not be listed below.

Work   Home   Church   Neighborhood   Bible study   PTA

Community social functions

· 2. If you circled one or added one of your own, write down why you think in this setting you are more prone to wear a mask.

Restored Vessels

Part of the challenge of our brokenness is to train our hearts to hear God's love above the din of our shame.

—Sheila, p.62

In chapter 3, we took a look at the Fall and the shame that resulted for Adam and Eve. Shame often makes us hide, and we want to cover ourselves.

• 3. Read Genesis 3:9–10. What did Adam confess to God?

As Christians living on this side of the cross, we still have an instinct to hide from God. What sin have you tried to carry yourself, thinking it is too big for God?

Because of the saving work of Christ, we don't have to hide *from* God, but can hide *in* God instead. When we seek the Lord's presence we are safe. Believing that your sin is too great for God to reconcile rejects the power of the cross.

Read Hebrews 4:14–16.

High Priest: a chief priest of the Hebrew people traced back to Aaron. He was distinguished above the other priests and viewed as the spiritual head of God's people. Israel came to him to learn the will of God (Exodus 28:3).

• 4. Who is Jesus likened to in verse 14?
• 5. Verse 16 tells us that we should come _____ to the throne of God. And there we receive *mercy* and *grace*.
• 6. We learn in this passage that Jesus was tempted in all points as we are. We must not infer that life was easy for Him. Though He was without sin, how does this human experience make it easier to approach Him?
• 7. Read Hebrews 5:5. How does this verse reveal Jesus' humility as God's appointed High Priest?
• 8. What does Hebrews 7:24–25 tell us about Jesus' priesthood?

Under the old system, the high priest went to God on behalf of his people. Under the new covenant we can come boldly and directly. Mediation is no longer necessary. We are assured that we can drop the masks we hide behind and seek the presence of God. Jesus was with God when the universe was made and from the power of His Word rules the heavens. Yet He can sympathize with us, too, because He willingly left His Father's throne to take on flesh. Jesus has conquered sin, showing Himself to be fully God and fully man.

Stepping-Stones

One thing that keeps us close to God is confession. We don't have to hide our sins from Him—He knows them all anyway. When we seek His forgiveness and thank Him for it, it is easier to receive His grace.

- 9. Write down one sin that you have tried to keep hidden, maybe even from yourself. After you have written it down, read again Hebrews 4:14–16. Take time to praise and thank Him for the mercy and grace that He freely gives today.

You don't have to hide anymore. You are loved as you are. You needn't wear a mask; God sees you as you are. You don't have to pretend to be okay; Christ is our righteousness, and we get to be human after all, to be real, to be loved, to be free. You don't have to deny the truth; the Lord knows it all and offers you Christ.

—Sheila, p. 65

S I X

What Can I Know for Sure?

Three Rock-Solid Truths to Keep You Standing Whatever Happens

Broken Pieces

What can I know for sure? may be the most important question you have in your life right now. Maybe you're questioning God's love for you or struggling with some aspect of your faith. Maybe you are in a place where you are waiting on God's ultimate answer to a prayer. Maybe you just received news that has left you reeling.

- Write out your thoughts and complete each statement with a short paragraph.

    I have to trust God right now because I'm uncertain that:_____

    _____

    _____

    _____

    Though I'm unsure about my circumstances, I do know this is true of God:

    _____

    _____

    _____

Restored Vessels

In chapter 5, you read about the tension between shame and a loving God. This chapter study will focus on the sovereignty of God. As we live and maneuver around in a world that often forgets God's truth, we can be sure of *who* God is when everything else is changing right before our eyes. Though this world can have the appearance that everyone but God is ruling, this simply is not true. Scripture promises that He is the ultimate Ruler of this world. Even Satan and his fallen angels can only do what He allows for a time. Yes, even Satan is subject to God. The enemy cannot even begin to compare to the power of God.

Sovereignty: the unlimited power of God; God's control over the affairs of nature and history; supreme ruler.

Scripture declares that God is working out His sovereign plan of redemption, and the conclusion is certain: God wins. Though we have fallen short and sinned against God, His plan for us overrides our brokenness. His sovereignty is characterized by His justice and holiness.

Read the following scriptures on the sovereignty of God.

- 1. In your own words, write down what each passage means to you:
     Genesis 14:18–20
     Exodus 6:2
     Luke 2:29
     Acts 4:24
     Revelation 6:10

Nothing happens in this world that God doesn't know about, and so we know that whatever is a surprise to us is not a surprise to Him. He is prepared for all situations, and nothing challenges His control. As we break down what it means for God to be sovereign over good and evil, let's look at three of His divine attributes, also known as the three "omni" attributes. *Omni* is Latin for "all."

Read over His sovereign attributes:

- 2. God is omnipotent (all-powerful)
     Mark 14:36
     Luke 1:37
     Because my God is all-powerful, I can be sure that _____

     _____.

The greatest single distinguishing feature of the omnipotence of God is that our imagination gets lost when thinking about it.

—Blaise Pascal

- 3. God is omniscient (all-knowing)

  1 John 3:20

  John 21:17

  Isaiah 44:7–8

  Because my God knows all things, I can be sure that _____

  _____ .

God's knowledge is linked to his sovereignty: he knows each thing, both in itself and in relation to all other things, because he created it, sustains it, and now makes it function every moment according to his plan for it.

—J. I. Packer

- 4. God is omnipresent (everywhere all the time)

  Psalm 139:7–12

  Jeremiah 23:23–24

If God is present at every point in space, if we cannot go where He is not, cannot even conceive of a place where He is not, why then has not that Presence become the one universally celebrated fact of the world?

—A. W. Tozer

- 5. Which one of the three "omnis" means the most to you right now?

Remember the former things, those of long ago;
    I am God, and there is no other;
    I am God, and there is none like me.
I make known the end from the beginning,
    from ancient times, what is still to come.
I say: My purpose will stand,
    and I will do all that I please.

—Isaiah 46:9–10

Stepping-Stones

As you grapple with the unknowns of now and the future, remember this: He knows your life, your history, and what is to come, too—right down to the tiniest detail. God knows what is still to come in *your* life, and He declares to you that His purpose for you will stand. In *your* life He will do everything that pleases Him.

Philippians 4:6–7 can strengthen us as we forge ahead into unforeseen outcomes: "Do not be anxious about anything, but in everything by prayer and supplication with thanksgiving let your requests be made known to God. And the peace of God, which surpasses all understanding, will guard your hearts and your minds in Christ Jesus" (ESV).

Personalize this passage and fill in the blanks:

I will not be anxious about _____ but I will pray about every-thing and give thanks to God and tell Him _____. Then I'm promised that His peace, which surpasses my understanding, will guard my heart and mind in Christ Jesus.

A Tale of Two Teresas
Time-Tested Wisdom for Dealing with Persistent Pain

Broken Pieces

You may or may not be familiar with Mother Teresa's writings, but most everyone remembers her as a self-sacrificing nun who deeply loved God and others. Reread her letter to Jesus:

> Lord, my God, who am I that You should forsake me? The Child of your Love—and now become as the most hated one—the one—You have thrown away as unwanted—unloved. I call, I cling, I want—and there is no One to answer—no One on Whom I can cling—no, No One.—Alone. . . . Where is my Faith—even deep down right in there is nothing, but emptiness & darkness—My God—how painful is this unknown pain -I have no Faith—I dare not utter the words & thoughts that crowd in my heart—& make me suffer untold agony.
>
> So many unanswered questions live within me afraid to uncover them—because of the blasphemy—If there be God—please forgive me—When I try to raise my thoughts to Heaven—there is such convicting emptiness that those very thoughts return like sharp knives & hurt my very soul.—I am told God loves me—and yet the reality of darkness & coldness & emptiness is so great that nothing touches my soul.

• 1. Have you ever felt like the darkness around you was so strong that it seemed more powerful than God? Explain.

I pray that your "dark night" doesn't stretch to such extreme lengths. I pray that the dawn comes soon—the merest hint of gray on the eastern horizon that blossoms into a lovely new sunrise in your life.

—Sheila, p. 81

Restored Vessels

John the Baptist—forerunner of Jesus, who brought good news about the coming Messiah; both Jesus and John were named by Gabriel, even before their birth; John's boyhood years are unknown, much like Jesus' early years; John and Jesus were born just months apart and were cousins; all four Gospels speak of John living "in the wilderness"; John understood his ministry to be one of reform and preparing people to receive Jesus as Messiah (Matthew 3).

Read Matthew 11:1–6

- 1. Even Jesus' closest followers became discouraged and doubted God's plan. What question does John the Baptist raise while he is in prison (see also Matthew 3:11)?
- 2. Read Matthew 3:1–6. In light of Matthew 11:1–6, and knowing what John the Baptist's calling was, do you think his doubts are reasonable?
- 3. How does Jesus respond to John's question?
- 4. How did God publicly endorse Jesus, according to Acts 2:22?

In this chapter, the two Teresas struggled with their feelings and chose to live beyond them. They didn't allow pain or darkness to separate them from God. When we think of Mother Teresa, we think of a life sacrificed to help the destitute, generously giving her smiles and love, though in reality she felt destitute in her own soul. And it is like God to raise up a woman like Teresa of Avila to write on prayer, the very thing she professed to despise.

In the midst of our brokenness, no matter how we feel, we must make an effort to commune with God. We may be angry, disappointed, disillusioned, and weary. But we exercise our faith anyway, which is not rooted in our feelings but in faithful trust of the Father.

Read this honest prayer of David:

My God, My God, why have You forsaken Me?
Why are You so far from helping Me,
And from the words of My groaning?
O My God, I cry in the daytime, but You do not hear;
And in the night season, and am not silent.

But You are holy,
Enthroned in the praises of Israel.
Our fathers trusted in You;
They trusted, and You delivered them.
They cried to You, and were delivered;
They trusted in You, and were not ashamed.

But I am a worm, and no man;
A reproach of men, and despised by the people.
All those who see Me ridicule Me;
They shoot out the lip, they shake the head, saying,
"He trusted in the LORD, let Him rescue Him;
Let Him deliver Him, since He delights in Him!"

But You are He who took Me out of the womb;
You made Me trust while on My mother's breasts.
I was cast upon You from birth.
From My mother's womb
You have been My God.
Be not far from Me,
For trouble is near;
For there is none to help.

(PSALM 22:1–11 NKJV)

This psalm is about anguish and abandonment. But it is about joy and God's reign too. King David won countless battles with God on his side. David, a mighty warrior, saw victory against all military odds because of

God's power and faithfulness to His people. Miracles definitely point to God's authority, and sometimes remembering what God has brought us through will build up our faith, so we can remember His provision and have confidence He will carry us through yet another trial.

David felt abandoned. John the Baptist felt abandoned. According to the passages studied, how do they deal with these real and legitimate feelings?

What is your first response when you feel like God has abandoned you?

Stepping-Stones

Reflect on the two Teresas mentioned in this chapter. Both understood what it felt like to suffer and long for more of God's presence in their lives. In our humanness, we can convince ourselves that our prayers won't make a difference, though Scripture is clear that our prayers are powerful and effective (James 5:16).

Most of us have felt like these two Teresas or like Naomi, when we are certain God has raised His fist against us (Ruth 1:13). Circle the sentiment that best describes your thoughts when you are in the midst of feeling abandoned by God:

"It doesn't matter if I pray. God will do what He wants anyway."

"I don't have the energy to pray, and why should I pray if my heart isn't in it?"

"Scripture says to pray without ceasing. Because of my conviction that God's Word is true, I pray, even when I'm discouraged."

As Christians, we must remember that God is not afraid of our feelings. He welcomes them and wants us to tell Him about everything. Finish this study by writing down something you are discouraged about. Then close with words of praise to God, and proclaim your trust to Him, even in the dark.

EIGHT

FIERCE LOVE AND HALLOWEEN GRACE

Why God's Ferocious Commitment to You Comes with Surprises

Broken Pieces

God's love is a topic that cannot be exhausted. As we grow in our walk with Him, we will discover more and more how big and fierce His love is for us. And all of us experience His love in different ways because as broken people, we all need a different touch.

· 1. Describe your understanding of God's love for you. Try and use words that communicate your personal experience, not just what you know from Scripture.
· 2. What imagery comes to mind when you think about the phrase "unconditional love" used to describe God's love for us?

> *I worry that by constantly using the phrase—and seldom explaining what we mean by it—we've robbed it of its original force. People today hear it and tend to think that when they sin against the Lord, He'll respond, "It's okay, don't worry about it. I'll love you anyway," when I think He really responds with something more like, "I'll love you forever, and that's why it's not okay."*

—Sheila, p. 92

Restored Vessels

God's love cannot be fully comprehended. His love often leaves us confused for a time. One of the hardest passages for believers and nonbelievers alike is the story of Abraham and Isaac.

Read Genesis 22:1–14.

- 3. As you reflect on this passage, know that Abraham was also in the dark as he followed God to Mount Moriah. How does this passage leave you in the dark?
- 4. There are three strong imperatives from God in this story: "Take," "go," and "sacrifice him." In what ways did these words stretch Abraham beyond what he thought he could bear? Does God explain why?
- 5. What did Abraham learn about God's love through his trust in God?
- 6. In verse 7, who raises the question "Where is the lamb?"

In the darkest hours of Abraham's life, he is able to say, "The Lord will provide" in a way that he had never known before. He didn't say these words to calm his son; rather, he knew he could depend on God in the dramatic last moments. After traveling fifty miles, not knowing how this would be reconciled, Abraham displayed his own fierce love for God. Abraham knew that God opposed the pagan human sacrifices that were practiced (Leviticus 20:1–5), so none of it made any sense to him. Though there was no lamb in sight.

- 7. Abraham named the site of the altar, Yahweh-Yireh. What does it mean (see v. 14)?
- 8. Refer to the benefits of suffering on pages 102–3. Through suffering, God will restore, establish, strengthen, and settle us. Write out how God did this for Abraham through his testing.

Restore

kartarizein

Establish

sterixein

Strengthen

sthenoun

Settle

themelioun

And behold, the word of the LORD came to him, saying, "This one shall not be your heir, but one who will come from your own body shall be your heir." Then He brought him outside and said, "Look now toward heaven, and count the stars if you are able to number them." And He said to him, "So shall your descendants be."

And he believed in the LORD, and He accounted it to him for righteousness.

(Genesis 15:4–6 NKJV)

Stepping-Stones

We have many examples in the Bible of broken people who endured profound suffering. Hebrews 11 is full of such people. As you read through the list, you may also be aware of their major mess ups and character flaws. Yet God used them in mighty ways to reveal His goodness. God's love does take us to places we didn't ask to go with Him, yet when we obey, His love is bigger and more alive than we ever thought possible. Abraham was called a "friend of God" in Scripture because of his faith, and much of Hebrews 11 is dedicated to this patriarch. If he had not trusted God, he would not know His love in such an intimate, saving way.

· 9. Draw a "road" that God took you on where all you could do is trust. Yours might have been more than a three-day trek like Abraham's; maybe you have been a few years on this unknown road. Mark it with symbols that show "the Lord provided" in ways you did not expect. What would you name the final destination?

There is something doubly precious about a faith which has come victoriously through pain and sorrow and disappointment. The wind will extinguish a weak flame; but it will fan a strong flame into a still greater blaze. So it is with faith.

—William Barclay, p. 103

Nine

Nothing to Protect, Nothing to Lose

Three Choices When Suffering Moves You from the Balcony to the Stage

Broken Pieces

Choice is something God gives us, and sometimes we do choose our own way, thinking it will keep us from suffering. But usually it means we miss out on a blessing God has for us.

- 1. Think about a time when you willfully chose to go your own way and later saw the missed blessing. How did this impact your relationship with God?

Read through the scriptures below that ask us to make a choice toward God's ways. Circle the one you are choosing to do today, though it may be hard.

- "Let us not become weary in doing good, for at the proper time we will reap a harvest if we do not give up" (Galatians 6:9).
- "Let the peace of Christ rule in your hearts, since as members of one body you were called to peace. And be thankful" (Colossians 3:15).
- "Let us then approach the throne of grace with confidence, so that we may receive mercy and find grace to help us in our time of need" (Hebrews 4:16).
- "Let us hold unswervingly to the hope we profess, for he who promised is faithful" (Hebrews 10:23).
- "Through Jesus, therefore, let us continually offer to God a sacrifice of praise—the fruit of lips that confess his name" (Hebrews 13:15).

Restored Vessels

Job—God's suffering saint. The book of Job is largely poetry and considered to be one of the Wisdom books in the Old Testament. This is an account of one faithful man's plight with suffering. Job is a model of spiritual integrity, though he, too, was broken. He held fast to his faith without understanding the reason for his suffering. Ultimately, through great loss and affliction, and through bad advice from friends, Job finally saw God's power with clarity, and he learned to trust in ways his mind doesn't even understand.

To state the purpose of the book of Job in one statement is difficult, as it is multifaceted. We see a look at reality that is much like our world: broken people responding to suffering; an honest man trying to submit to the will of God; the reality of Satan trying to discourage us and keep us from God's plan; and how humanity can clash with God's divine purposes. Job also illustrates that though we are often sinful, weak, and ignorant, we can be upright and purely devoted to God in the midst of facing adversity.

Read Job 1
- 1. What do we learn about Job's life in verses 1–5?
- 2. How do we know from verse 6 that God rules over all of evil?
- 3. How does God describe Job to Satan (v. 8)?
- 4. What losses did Job experience through the hand of Satan?
- 5. How does Job respond to his troubles, according to verse 20?
- 6. When we experience profound suffering, our natural tendency is to find someone to blame. Do you usually blame others, yourself, or God?

In all of this, Job did not sin by blaming God. (Job 1:22 NTL)

Read 2 Corinthians 1:3–7
- 7. What is Paul's charge to us when we face trouble?
- 8. What are the benefits of suffering according to Paul?

Stepping-Stones

My prayer is that you are finding it easier to embrace the reality of the brokenness in your own life. We don't have to fear it because God is using it all to draw us to Him. To summarize:

- Broken people have nothing to protect and nothing to lose.
- Broken people don't fear suffering, because they've chosen to use it to drive them into God's loving arms.
- Broken people don't fear men, because they know that who lives inside them is greater than whoever stands before them.
- Broken people don't fear death, because they know who and what awaits them on the other side.

How is God using your brokenness to set you free?

God uses broken things. It takes broken soil to produce a crop, broken clouds to give rain, broken grain to give bread, broken bread to give strength. It is the broken alabaster box that gives forth perfume. It is Peter, weeping bitterly, who returns to greater power than ever.

Streams in the Desert—p. 113

TEN

CALLED TO SOMETHING BIGGER
Allow God to Use Your Pain for Heaven's Stunning Purposes

Broken Pieces

Our walk with God is full of paradoxes. The worst day can end up being the best day. Sometimes darkness helps us see God's light all the more. God even uses the darkest and foul places to reveal His truth and beauty.

- 1. Think of a dark experience or place. How did God show up unexpectedly for you? Were you able to discern He was there right away or after it was over?

God delights in men and women reaching outside of themselves to do "great" things for others. He calls broken people not only to place their faith in Him, despite the darkness, but also to dare to reach beyond themselves and, through faith, bring the healing, loving touch of Christ to other hurting men and women.

—Sheila. p. 122

Restored Vessels

Earlier in our study, we looked at the great faith of the centurion. Jesus also said the Canaanite woman, an outcast, demonstrated great faith. Both of these stories were about Gentiles who were commended for their amazing faith in Christ. In Matthew 15, Jesus had now entered pagan territory. The author, Matthew, makes a point to mention her ancestry, which linked her to Israel's enemies—the Canaanites, people against the God of Israel who worshipped many pagan gods. Once again, Jesus shows the power of God to reconcile the least likely to the Messiah. No one is beyond the reach of God.

Read Matthew 15:21–28

- 2. How did Jesus respond to her request at first? How did the disciples respond?
- 3. Though He was in Gentile territory and healed other Gentiles, why did Jesus make a point to tell her He came for the lost sheep of Israel?
- 4. According to verse 25, what was this Gentile woman's reaction to Jesus' response?
- 5. Sometimes we compare our level of brokenness with others and convince ourselves, *Well, I can't reach out to this person; he is just too far gone to help*. Jesus proves throughout Scripture that there is no darkness that He cannot expel. No situation or place is void of His presence. How does the Canaanite woman's faith clearly penetrate the darkness of her lineage?

When Jesus speaks in verse 28, He speaks with great conviction and emotion: "Woman, you have great faith!" The text says her daughter was healed that very hour. After this, Matthew reveals more and more miracles that Jesus performs for Gentiles. The blessings begin to clearly flow for both Jew and Gentile. Like the Jews, sometimes we believe only certain circles of people deserve to receive God's love. But the truth is, none of us deserve God's grace. All of us are in the same boat—we are indeed broken. The answer for all of us is to rely on Him to make up for what we lack, which begins to overflow in our lives when we spend time with Him. Like the Canaanite woman, we need to kneel before Jesus and worship Him.

Make a point to do the following:

- 6. Pray and read. Read Ephesians 3:3–4 and write out what it means in your own words.

- 7. Pray and study. Read 2 Timothy 2:15 and write out what it means in your own words.

• 8. Pray and ransack. Read Proverbs 2:3–5 and write out what it means in your own words.

• 9. Pray and think. Read 2 Timothy 2:7 and write out what it means in your own words.

Stepping-Stones

When we truly embrace the darkness that surrounds us, our own brokenness doesn't have to be something we are afraid of. God can handle it, and there is freedom when we let go of trying to compensate for what we lack. We need to exercise our faith in Him, not in us. Write down something in your life that you know weighs down on you.

• 10. Close this study by writing out your prayer of faith. Take comfort in the fact you can start with, "Lord, I believe, help my unbelief!" (Mark 9:24 NKJV). End with words of belief that He is setting you free.

Growing in Christ means letting go of our need to understand or control everything, and letting go of our need for approval. The closer we approach the heart of Christ, the less our faith becomes about us, about what makes us feel good, and the more it becomes about others.

—Sheila, p. 123

ONLY THE WOUNDED CAN SERVE
What If Your Wounds Make You Fit for
His Service?

Broken Pieces

Perhaps through this study you have been able to be more open with your-self and God about your wounds, whether brought about through your own mistakes or through living in a fallen world. Our wounds truly can be a blessing in disguise.

• Think about a wound you carry and fill in the blanks:

If I had not suffered _____ I wouldn't know that God can ____
_____.

Though I wouldn't wish my suffering on anyone, I'm thankful I can help others who _____.

In love's service only the wounded soldiers can serve.
—Thornton Wilder

Restored Vessels

Born as a Roman citizen, Paul had a Jewish heritage that meant more to him than anything. Studying under Gamaliel, a renowned rabbi of the day, Paul was being well-grounded in Jewish orthodoxy.

As the gospel was spreading, Paul set out to persecute Christians and wanted them killed. Paul associated himself with Stephen's executioners (the first martyr recorded in Scripture) and then began on his mission to kill Christ followers. With great confidence in the law, he then was confronted with the person of Jesus. There are three accounts of Paul's conversion in Acts: chapters 9, 22, and 26.

The apostle Paul is credited to have written about two-thirds of the New Testament. His story speaks to what God can do with the least likely of men. Even Paul called himself the "least of the apostles" (1 Corinthians 15:9), yet probably no other Christian has had the influence of Paul. We will never know this side of heaven how many have come to faith when reading one of Paul's letters. His writings are still bringing people to Christ.

Read Acts 9:1–19

- 1. How does the story open up in verses 1–2? What was Saul (later called Paul) doing?
- 2. Clearly, we see that Saul felt confident with his ancestral faith. He didn't realize his own need for a Savior and was spiritually blind to the condition of his soul. Think back to a time when you were not aware of your spiritual depravity. How did God expose it to you?
- 3. Review verses 4–7. After the light from heaven fell on Saul, what did Jesus say to him? How did Saul respond?
- 4. Review verses 10–19. God had supplied the right Christians to be around Paul in his time of need. What was Ananias's first reaction in reaching out to Paul?
- 5. God uses other believers to help us see our brokenness. We all need a safe place to heal and to be vulnerable. When has God provided you the right friend at the right time to help you "see" better?

Damascus: a large and thriving commercial center near a mountain range. The city had a large Jewish population and had been part of the Roman province of Syria since 64 BC.

- 6. Paul's conversion story illustrates our complete dependence on God. Even though Paul was deceived, God showed mercy and met him on the Damascus Road, shattering his spiritual blindness. Paul didn't deserve this miracle—Jesus came to him anyway. Think about someone in your life who you know doesn't even realize she is broken, in need of Jesus. How can you be Ananias to her?

After Paul's conversion, he set out to evangelize both Gentiles and Jews, largely Gentiles. With that, he was promised suffering (Acts 9:16). Throughout his letters, Paul describes his sufferings and losses, but counts them as nothing compared to his salvation in Christ.

Read over the following afflictions that Paul endured:

I have worked harder than any of them. I have served more prison sentences! I have been beaten times without number. I have faced death again and again.

I have been beaten the regulation thirty-nine stripes by the Jews five times.

I have been beaten with rods three times. I have been stoned once. I have been shipwrecked three times. I have been twenty-four hours in the open sea.

In my travels I have been in constant danger from rivers and floods, from bandits, from my own countrymen, and from pagans. I have faced danger in city streets, danger in the desert, danger on the high seas, danger among false Christians. I have known exhaustion, pain, long vigils, hunger and thirst, going without meals, cold and lack of clothing.

Apart from all external trials I have the daily burden of responsibility for all the churches . . . .

In Damascus, the town governor, acting by King Aretas' order had men out to arrest me. I escaped by climbing through a window and being let down the wall in a basket. That's the sort of dignified exit I can boast about. (2 Corinthians 11:23–28, 32–33 PHILLIPS)

- 7. List the afflictions he endured:
- 8. Paul's life is stunning, as he knew that suffering was temporal and fruit would come. What fruit can you see from Paul's endurance? How about your own?

Stepping-Stones

Galatians 6:2 says, "Bear one another's burdens, and so fulfill the law of Christ" (ESV). There are seasons in our lives when God does take us to a place of rest and healing. But this is usually just a season. We are meant to give back to one another because God also knows it benefits the body of Christ.

We've come a long way in our candid discussion about brokenness. I pray that God is stirring you now to reach out to someone with a similar wound to yours. Paul knew, too, that when we've suffered, we then can show compassion in a way we wouldn't be able to without experiencing it firsthand.

- 9. Think about someone you know who is hurting. Ask God to give you strength to reach out. You may feel very inadequate, but keep your eyes on the One who is more than adequate. Write out what you want them to know about you that may lead them toward His healing touch.

Are you tired? Worn out? Burned out on religion? Come to me. Get away with me and you'll recover your life. I'll show you how to take a real rest. Walk with me and work with me—watch how I do it. Learn the unforced rhythms of grace. I won't lay anything heavy or ill-fitting on you. Keep company with me and you'll learn to live freely and lightly.

—Matthew 11:28–30 *THE MESSAGE*

TWELVE

THE SACRED ACHE

How God Transforms Your Hurts into Something Holy

Broken Pieces

There isn't anything good in pain by itself. Pain that we don't entrust to God remains just what it is—pain. Because there are many factors in life that are uncontrollable, we cannot avoid it. Sometimes it isn't always easy to discern the source of our pain, whether it is wrong choices, consequences of living in a fallen world, or God's discipline. It's easy to want to ignore it and pretend it isn't there, but God wants us to be honest with Him.

- 1. Take a moment to listen to your heart. Do you sense a dull ache or maybe you feel intense pain? Complete the following statement:

  The source of my pain is _____.
  I'm trusting God to _____.

- 2. In your own words, describe what you think the *sacred ache* means.

  Pain is just pain. But when we choose to take that pain and present it to God for His sovereign use, then that pain becomes sacred. *Yes, we all have to deal with pain in the course of our lives—physical, emotional, and spiritual pain. But if we give God access to this pain, asking Him to turn it into something He can use . . . something happens. Something supernatural.*

  —Sheila, p. 141

Restored Vessels

The Bible gives us 150 psalms that are full of prayers, praise, revelation, and truth. The Greek word *psalmos* means "songs sung with accompaniment." We have responses to God from His people and God's responses to His people. Through them, we are invited to experience God for ourselves and walk with Him through every twist and turn we encounter here on earth. We hear God speak to His people as well as God's people speaking to Him. Quickly we see that there was freedom to express frustration, impatience, hurt, anger, and pain. The book of Psalms shows how God sees the individual as well as community.

Read Psalm 6

- 1. David is the author of Psalm 6. How does he show his honesty in the psalm?
- 2. David prays that the Lord will not discipline him only with justice, but with mercy too. What question does he ask God in verse 3?
- 3. Sometimes pain comes from the angst of waiting, the unknown. Write down a time when you felt that not knowing was even harder than hearing bad news.
- 4. In verse 5, David reminds God that the dead cannot remember Him. For David remembering involved praise for what God had done. In his pain, he doesn't deny God's worthiness of praise. Write down what you are grateful for, even in the midst of pain.
- 5. David mentions his anguish is more intense because for him it feels like no one has regard for his pain. In the moment of his suffering, he turns it over to God. In what line of the psalm do you think David turns his pain into *a sacred ache*?
- 6. Even through the pain, what does David acknowledge in verses 8–9?

Stepping-Stones

We can take great comfort in knowing that God is fully aware of every tear we have cried. Think about Jerry crying for forty days straight after his loss—that is a lot of tears. But Scripture tells us God saves our tears. He redeems all things. Nothing is wasted. God promised to keep track of all of our sorrows:

You keep track of all my sorrows.
You have collected all my tears in your bottle.
You have recorded each one in your book.

(PSALM 56:8 NLT)

No human mind can conceive of God's record-keeping abilities. We can praise Him for His compassion over us. Jesus is forever faithful to fulfill His redemption plan. Paradise will one day soon be regained, and we will return to being completely whole as we look toward our future hope and home with Christ (Revelation 21:4). God promises to redeem all that the enemy has tried to take from us. The great news is our current suffering is temporary. In light of eternity, it is all but a flicker of darkness.

Pain can keep us from God if we allow it. Revisit what you wrote down as your source of pain at the beginning of this chapter study. Use the word/phrase to fill in the blank below. Because He has promised to turn our sorrow to joy, fill in the redeemed version of your pain, whether you have received it or are waiting for it.

· He has turned my

_____ to _____.
(source of pain)   (source of joy)

THIRTEEN

CHRIST THE BROKEN

The Savior Who Chose Suffering . . . for You

Broken Pieces

Some churches celebrate Communion every Sunday, some quarterly, and others monthly. Some traditions such as Catholic, Eastern Orthodox, and Lutheran use the term *Eucharist*, which is a Greek term meaning "thanksgiving." Others use the word *Communion*, which means "fellowship." Before the Reformation, the Lord's Supper was central to a worship service—not the sermon. Every Sunday was a time to celebrate His power over the cross. Christ was the center focus of worship through the Lord's Supper.

It is easy to take Communion without entering into this miracle. On the night of Jesus' betrayal, before breaking the bread He gave thanks to the Father (Matthew 26:26). We see Jesus' incredible love for His Father here, as He is giving thanks for His suffering, that His body was about to be broken.

• 1. Write down a Communion experience that was particularly meaningful to you. What was God speaking to you during that time of worship?

"This is My body, broken for you."

He was born in poverty and died in disgrace and thought it well worthwhile.

—Dorothy Sayers

Restored Vessels

The one thing Satan knows is that Jesus won over sin and death through the power of His blood and the resurrection. This is something he doesn't want us to remember. This is why Jesus said, "Do this in remembrance of me." He doesn't ever want us to forget the power of the cross and that He has the answer to our brokenness. He doesn't want us to forget that He has all the help we need. We truly have overcome sin, death, and brokenness because of His sacrifice for us. Yet it is so easy to forget this truth, to take it for granted, and to not draw from its power in our daily lives. The more we "remember" what He did for us, the more we will believe in His power to resurrect our daily lives.

Read John 19:28–37

- 2. What were Jesus' last words before He bowed His head?
- 3. What do Jesus' last words mean to you personally?
- 4. A crucified man usually had his legs broken to hasten death. If the legs were broken, he couldn't raise his body to obtain a full breath. Why did the execution squad decide not to break Jesus' legs?
- 5. Read Psalm 34:20. Write out this prophecy fulfilled:

Broken people need to know that God keeps His word, even down to the smallest detail. So many of us have watched lies destroy our homes and broken promises shatter our lives. But this seemingly minor guarantee that God would allow no one to break the Messiah's bones shouts to me that I can trust Him in all things, both the big and the small. And therefore I glory in the words of Paul: "For no matter how many promises God has made, they are 'Yes' in Christ" (2 Corinthians 1:20).

—Sheila, pp.158–59

- 6. Read Isaiah 53:4–5 (NLT):

> *Yet it was our weaknesses he carried;*
> *it was our sorrows that weighed him down.*
> *And we thought his troubles were a punishment from God,*
> *a punishment for his own sins!*
> *But he was pierced for our rebellion,*
> *crushed for our sins.*

He was beaten so we could be whole.
He was whipped so we could be healed.

• 7. The cross is where God's power clearly conquers. How does this change how you view your brokenness?

Isaiah calls Jesus the Suffering Servant. His suffering was profound, and so often we want to skip over Good Friday to get to Resurrection Sunday. But we miss the power of His brokenness for us when we turn away from Jesus' pain. Though sinless, He knew the weight of sin as He hung on the cross and bore it for us. His Father in heaven knew He would overcome so we might have eternal life and the resurrection power in us. He knew His Son would accomplish His mission.

• 8. Look up 1 Peter 4:12–13—What two blessings come from suffering according to Peter?

I have _____ with Christ, and I should _____.

• 9. Look up Acts 14:22—We enter the _____ through suffering.

Stepping-Stones

You may have started this study feeling shame and guilt for being broken. Maybe you were in denial, but now you understand that Jesus understands and will carry you as you pick up the broken pieces of your life and offer them to God. Everyone is called to some type of suffering, and God our Maker knows what each of us is designed to carry. He knows our frame, He knows our weaknesses; He knows where we will go and who we will impact. What kind of brokenness has He called you to bear so that you might restore a brother or sister in need of healing? Remember God isn't wasteful, and He wants to use you as a vessel to bring healing to others.

• 10. Prayerfully write down what He is calling you to do with your brokenness that will help others. Attach a scripture to reinforce this, whether from previous chapters or one to reflect how you will serve Him in the days to come.

Closing Prayer

Father, I thank You for sending Your Son, Jesus, to heal our wounds, to set us free. I thank You that our story doesn't end in brokenness, but rather we are overcomers through Jesus Christ. Your broken body was and still is the answer to our broken lives. So, Lord, we offer You all the broken pieces and follow You with confidence. You have made us whole. In Jesus' name. Amen.

Notes

1. John Piper, *Desiring God: Tenth Anniversary Expanded Edition* (Sisters, OR: Multnomah Press, 1996), 23.
2. Clive James, *As of This Writing* (New York: W. W. Norton & Company, 2003), 127.
3. Edward J. Young, *The Book of Isaiah, Volume 3* (Grand Rapids, MI: William B. Eerdmans Publishing Company, 1972), 41.
4. Beth Moore, *Breaking Free* (Nashville: Broadman &Holman, 2000), 113.
5. "Dog Finds His Way Home After Alabama Tornado" http://abcnews.go.com/US/hero-dog-crawls-home-broken-legs-tornado-rubble/story?id=13703041.
6. C. S. Lewis, *The Four Loves* (New York: Harcourt Brace, 1991),121.
7. Moore, *Breaking Free*, 113–14.
8. Lewis Smedes, *Shame and Grace* (New York: HarperOne, 1994), 28.
9. "Shame" in *The International Standard Bible Encyclopedia*, vol. 4 (Grand Rapids, MI: William B. Eerdmans Publishing Company, 1988), 447.
10. Luis Palau, *Where Is God When Bad Things Happen?* (New York: Doubleday, 1999), 183–84.
11. Adapted from the Dallas Theological Seminary website.
12. Richard Foster, *Prayer: Finding the Heart's True Home* (New York: Harper Collins, 1992). 242.
13. W. McDonald and A. Farstad, *Believer's Bible Commentary: Old and New Testaments* (Mt 27:46) (Nashville: Thomas Nelson, 1997).
14. Derek Kidner, Genesis, *Tyndale Old Testament Commentaries*, IVP, 1967, 74.
15. David Van Biema, "Mother Teresa's Crisis of Faith," *Time*, August 23, 2007. All quotes in this chapter come from Van Biema's article.
16. Clayton L. Berg Jr., from the Introduction to *A Life of Prayer by St. Teresa of Avila* (Portland, OR: Multnomah Press, 1983), xix–xxxiv. The quotations in this section are all from Berg.
17. Teresa of Avila, *Interior Castle*, ed. E. Allison Peers (New York: Doubleday Image Books, 1961).
18. Brennan Manning, *The Ragamuffin Gospel* (Sisters, OR: Multnomah Publishers, 2005), 39–40.
19. C. S. Lewis, *The Lion, the Witch and the Wardrobe* (New York: Collier Books, 1950), 75–76.
20. Ibid., 180.
21. Richard Vincent, www.theocentric.com,
22. Steve Brown, *A Scandalous Freedom* (West Monroe, LA: Howard Publishing Company, 2004), 216.
23. See Genesis 32:22–32; Psalm 119:71; Matthew 14:15–21; 2 Corinthians 12:7–9.
24. William Barclay, *The Letters of James and Peter*, Revised Edition, (Westminster John Knox Press, 2003), 273–74.
25. Ibid., 274.
26. L. B. Cowman, *Streams in the Desert*, October 25, 1925 edition.
27. See 1 Samuel 13:14; Acts 13:22.
28. Dr. Henry Cloud, *Changes That Heal* (Grand Rapids, MI: Zondervan, 1990), 317.
29. *Expositor's Bible Commentary*, vol. 12. Hebrews 2:10(Grand Rapids, MI: Zondervan, 1992).
30. "Snow Stories: Sheep Have Forgotten How to Cope with Snow," *Télegraph*, July 14, 2011.
31. John Piper, *A Godward Life, Book Two* (Sisters, OR: Multnomah Books, 1999), 182–84.
32. Joni Eareckson Tada, *Heaven: Your Real Home* (Grand Rapids, MI: Zondervan, 1995), 187.
33. Thornton Wilder, *The Collected Short Plays of Thornton Wilder*, vol. 2. (New York: Theatre Communications group, 1998), 74.
34. Ibid., 75.
35. See Exodus 3:11.
36. Jerry Sittser, *A Grace Disguised*, exp ed. (Grand Rapids, MI: Zondervan, 2004), 27.

37. Ibid., 17–18.
38. Steve Brown, *A Scandalous Freedom* (West Monroe, LA: Howard Publishing, 2004), 197.
39. Sittser, *Grace Disguised*, 18.
40. Ibid., 193.
41. Ibid., 199.
42. Ibid.
43. Leigh McLeroy, *The Beautiful Ache* (Grand Rapids, MI: Fleming H. Revell, 2007), 13–14.
44. Ibid.
45. Kari Lundberg in *Protraits in Courage*, by Dave and Jan Dravecky (Grand Rapids, MI: Zondervan, 1998), 125.
46. Ibid., 126.
47. Ibid., 128.
48. Ibid.
49. Sittser, *Grace Disguised*, 205.
50. Ibid., 209.
51. Ibid., 212.
52. Adapted from the sermon "Mary," by Tim Keller, preached December 23, 2001, at Redeemer Presbyterian Church, New York, New York.
53. Dorothy Sayers, *Christian Letters to a Post-Christian World* (Grand Rapids, MI: Eerdmans, 1969), 14.

If you enjoyed *God Loves Broken People,* check out these other great books from gifted Bible teacher and inspiring Women of Faith® speaker Sheila Walsh.

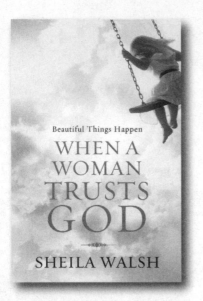

Beautiful Things Happen When A Woman Trusts God
God comes not to get us out of our difficulties, but to live in us through them.

Let Go
You *can* lay down your burdens. You *can* rest. You *can* find Peace. You *can* live free.